GW01402723

Single Chance

Single Dads of Dragonfly Lake

Amy Knupp

Copyright © 2025 by Amy Knupp

All rights reserved.

This is a work of fiction. Names, characters, places, and incidents are the product of the author's imagination and are used fictitiously. Any resemblances to actual events, locales, or persons living or dead, is purely coincidental.

No part of this book may be reproduced in any form or by any electronic or mechanical means, including information storage and retrieval systems, without written permission from the author, except for the use of brief quotations in a book review.

Chapter One

Rowan

As I opened the door to the noisy, crowded ballroom of the Honeysuckle Inn on New Year's Eve, a seed of optimism took root in me for the first time in more than two years.

I needed this. So badly. Needed to have fun, forget reality for a few hours, and immerse myself in happy people.

The beat of the music pounded through me. Shimmers of light from a disco ball shifted over every person and surface. The energy of the party enveloped me, making me feel alive even before I fully entered the room.

"Hello. Got your ticket?" a guy in a Luigi costume asked as my eyes adjusted to the dimness.

"Oh," I said. "I just checked into the inn tonight. Ava invited me. She loaned me this costume."

He looked me up and down briefly and tilted his head.

"Claire from *The Breakfast Club*," I told him.

"I was getting there," he said with a smile. "Red hair would complete it."

"Last minute," I explained. "Do you need to talk to Ava?"

"Nah. Welcome," Luigi said. "Happy New Year, eighties version." He gestured me past him.

I stepped to the left, where I spotted a bar. I'd need a drink—actually I was overdue for one hell of a bender—but first, a moment.

Taking in the scene, I breathed. Like, took a chest-lifting inhalation that filled my lungs fuller than they'd been in... months.

There was a live band at one end, playing a Culture Club song. People were stacked about fifteen deep around the stage, dancing and giving the musicians their full attention.

In one corner was a neon-green sign that said Arcade and several full-sized arcade games, each of them in use. In the center of the ballroom was more of a traditional dance floor with a few couples and a group of women on it. Opposite of where I stood, a neon-orange sign said Trivia.

Every corner was filled with people. People who didn't know me, didn't know what I'd been through. People who wouldn't scrutinize me to figure out whether a sympathetic look or a hug would be better received.

I was so tired of needing sympathy. Of my eyes filling with tears at an empathetic smile.

Even when I'd met Ava, the inn owner, at the check-in desk, more damn tears had threatened. The upside was that, as soon as she noticed, she'd stopped asking conversational, well-meaning questions about where I was from and what I was doing at the inn.

I sucked in another life-affirming breath.

Festive people. Upbeat music.

Freedom.

I needed all of it even more than I'd realized.

In the next second, a pang of guilt jabbed at me, but I shook it off.

Tonight was about looking ahead, not mourning the past.

This town might turn out to be my future, at least my short-term future. My respite. My chance to rediscover myself and focus on *my* life.

Drink, Rowan. You need a drink, girl.

At the bar, I ordered one of the eighties cocktails, a Blue Lagoon. It tasted like a blue vodka lemonade and had a festive curl of lemon peel floating on top.

It'd been months since I'd dared to try to relax with anything alcoholic. Now I carried my drink to a spot along the wall and took a sip. I let the sweetness and the distinct taste of alcohol sit on my tongue for several seconds. My eyes fluttered shut in appreciation.

When I opened them, my attention caught on a guy at the bar whose gaze was on me. He smiled, and I felt a pulse of something I hadn't felt in ages.

Interest.

He was tall with dark hair and broad shoulders under a light brown trench coat. What tripped up my heart was that smile. It reached across the room and grabbed me.

I smiled back, then glanced away self-consciously, resisting the urge to check behind me to verify it was actually *me* he'd been looking at.

I was out of practice on more than enjoying a cocktail. I hadn't been on a date for over three years, since the early days with Christian. Hadn't been with a man since he'd dumped me because of my inability to give him enough of my time, or really, *any* of my time, once I'd become my grandmother's full-time caretaker.

Alzheimer's was like that. It not only robbed its victims of their brain, identity, and life but also took so much from the victims' loved ones. I didn't regret a single minute with my grandmother, felt genuinely grateful I'd been her trusted one at her side as she gradually transitioned out of a long, love-filled life. But recovery would take a while. Finding my way forward would be a process.

My next breath was shaky, and I had to force my grandmother, my grief, and my profound loss out of my mind.

Not tonight.

Tonight was about possibilities.

I glanced around for the guy from the bar. He was no longer there, and my gaze skimmed the room until I spotted him among a group of people gathered around several of the standing cocktail tables. At the same moment I saw him, he turned his head my way, and we made eye contact again.

There was the smile. He had an irresistible dimple on one side.

My heart raced, and a feeling of lightness rushed through my chest.

I lifted my glass for a drink and looked away, trying to play it cool.

As the band started a Billy Idol song, I meandered closer to the stage, sipping my drink and bobbing my head slightly to the beat. They were good. The lead singer had the Billy Idol growl down. The guitarist's hair was very eighties, like those guys from Duran Duran.

I was angled just enough to the side of the stage that I could easily, nonchalantly glance toward the brown-coat guy, and I'm not even kidding, he happened to look my way again.

I might be out of practice, but I was pretty sure he was checking me out.

I didn't hate it.

I also knew better than to come across as a desperate girl. I'd just gotten here, for Pete's sake. The outdated expression had been my grandmother's favorite and came to mind automatically, bringing with it a pang of sadness and a bittersweet smile.

I was a certifiable mess in my head. I didn't need to hook up with anyone. I just needed to enjoy the mental space. Savor the lack of responsibility.

I watched the band through three more songs, hovering along the wall so I wasn't really part of the crowd. When they went to intermission, I wandered toward a different bar, planning to order another Blue Lagoon. On the way, a guy dressed in a blue letterman jacket stopped me.

"Claire?"

"No," I said automatically. Then the blue letterman jacket of his costume clicked. "Oh! Andrew?" My counterpart from the movie.

We laughed and agreed we had to share a dance to the Go-Gos, played by the DJ who was spelling the band. Our conversation remained impersonal as we discussed the best lines of *The Breakfast Club*. The most personal we got was me confessing I was not, in fact, a princess, and him clarifying he'd never wrestled in his life but had played tennis and golf in high school.

At the end of the song, he leaned in and said, "Thank you for the dance, Claire. I'm off to find the goth basket-case chick for the next one."

I laughed and wished him luck, then resumed my path to the bar.

How long had it been since I'd danced? Just set aside reality for three minutes and felt the music?

Ages.

Dancing was good for the soul, I decided. I needed to dance more, even though I wasn't a particularly good dancer.

And laughter? Mine was almost rusty.

More dancing, more laughing.

More alcohol.

I resumed my path to the bar near the arcade, taking in the costumes and characters on my way. The eighties were before my time, but I'd fallen asleep to so many movies in the past two years that I'd seen at least pieces of all the big ones from that decade and beyond. I spotted a group of ninja turtles, a Ms. Pac-Man, the couple from *The Princess Bride*, Prince, and a lot I couldn't identify in a flash as I walked by.

This little town was going all out for its New Year's celebration.

I'd never been to Dragonfly Lake before, but Presley had promised me it was adorable and friendly and would make a good landing place. She'd arranged for me to meet her best friend, Chloe Henry, to discuss a possible job opening. I had no idea whether it would pan out, but I was grateful to have a starting point.

I waited in a short line at the bar, keeping my head down but my ears open. I was curious about this place but not up for meeting bunches of people. With each introduction would come questions I wasn't sure I could answer without getting emotional. My introverted self was content to be in the crowd but not too connected to it.

"What can I get for you?" the female bartender asked when it was my turn.

"A Blue Lagoon."

She tilted her head as I said it, studying my light pink blouse and white scarf. "The popular girl from *The Break-fast Club*?"

I nodded, impressed because she looked several years younger than my twenty-nine. "You got it."

When she handed over my drink, she said, "Good luck finding your bad boy."

I laughed as I turned around, then stopped short.

The brown-coat guy stood there, front and center, six feet from me, all his attention on me, holding a large boom box in both hands above his head. He was even better-looking this close, with one side of his mouth quirked up in a half grin and his warm, hopeful eyes gauging my reaction.

At once, I realized he was dressed as the guy from *Say Anything*, and the song the DJ had just started was "In Your Eyes" from the same movie.

I laughed self-consciously, and this time I did look behind me to make sure it was me his focus was aimed at. No one at the bar was paying attention to us, though a few people around him had noticed his bold antics and watched for my reaction.

I smiled, unsure what to do, but then he stepped forward and said, "Lloyd Dobler. Would you like to dance?"

The name jogged my memory as the movie's main character, so I replied, "Sure. I'm Claire."

"Lloyd" lowered the boom box and held out a hand toward me, smiling more fully, flashing me that dimple.

My insides dipped, and a spark pulsed through me as I took his hand. As he led me to the dance floor, he set the boom box aside on a table. I took a couple of swallows of my new cocktail, then set it next to the boom box. I wanted to dance more than I wanted that drink.

When he laced our fingers together, it felt natural, which was strange since I didn't even know his real name.

Once on the dance floor, we faced each other. He kept holding my right hand and slid his other hand to my back, above my waist. I rested my left hand on his shoulder, and we swayed to the in-between beat with just a couple of inches between us.

"You look old for high school," he said with a grin.

"High school?" Did he somehow know I was a high-school teacher? Then it hit me: He was still referring to my character. "Oh! Yes, well, you look too old for high school too, so I guess we have something in common."

We both laughed.

"You're not from Dragonfly Lake," he said.

I shook my head. "You must be if you know I'm not."

"I moved here a couple of years ago."

"I arrived after the sun went down, so I haven't even seen the town yet."

"Where are you from?"

"Nashville. Where did you move from?"

"I'm originally from St. Louis."

My brows went up. "You moved from there to this little town?"

He nodded. "When I was a kid, I went on vacation one summer with a buddy and his family to Dragonfly Lake. It left an impression, I guess."

I had so many questions, but I bit down on them. The more questions I asked him, the more he'd ask me, and I didn't have it in me to go into too many details, regardless of how attracted to him I was...and believe me, I was.

He was nearly half a foot taller than my five seven. His jaw was covered with a scruff of facial hair I wouldn't quite call a beard. His eyes were a milk-chocolate brown, with the beginnings of crinkles at the outer edges, telling me he laughed frequently. Beyond that, they were intent on me in a way that drew me in rather than made me feel uncomfortable.

The space between us lessened. I wasn't sure if it was my doing or his—or both. Our bodies were lightly touching now, and it awakened a pulse of desire deep within me. I breathed in his scent, picking up notes of wood and spice. It made me want to nestle up against him and soak in the feel of his protective arms and strong hands.

I'd never experienced this kind of instant, powerful attraction. Was it my vulnerable state? That I'd been on my own, without a man's touch, for so long? Was it the magic of costumes and make-believe and a guy who'd fake serenaded me with a boom box in the middle of a crowd?

Or was it just this particular man? This man whose name I realized I still didn't know.

I stopped overthinking, stopped questioning. I was exhausted on a soul level, and right now I had the opportunity to just *be* for the last two minutes of the song. To sink into the moment with this guy I was unquestionably drawn to and felt strangely safe with.

Next the DJ slowed the tempo down even more with "Take My Breath Away." My partner pulled me in closer, dropping my hand to put both of his on my back. I slid my hands to the nape of his neck, his coarse hair brushing over my fingers, and we swayed as one, our bodies flush.

We kept dancing through "Saving All My Love for You" and "Against All Odds," and then the DJ welcomed the band back for one more short set.

"Lloyd" took my hand, bent to my ear, and said, "How about a breather? I could show you your first view of the lake."

"On one condition," I said, more than ready for fresh air even though I knew it would be cold.

"Name it."

"Tell me your real name."

He flashed that dimpled smile down at me. "It's Chance." He raised his brows as if asking mine.

"I'm Rowan."

"That fits you better than Claire."

"Chance fits you a hundred times better than Lloyd," I said with a laugh.

He led me out of the ballroom onto the inn's terrace. The air was brisk but refreshing. The sudden quiet was a relief. I exhaled, sending a visible puff into the cold air.

"Here." Chance took off his trench coat, stepped behind me, and held it out for me to put on.

"Then you'll get cold," I said, taking in his T-shirt and cargo pants.

"I'm good," he said, so I slid the coat on and pulled it around me, noticing it smelled like him.

"Thank you." Still secretly inhaling the smell of his coat, I took in the scene before me.

A string of lights lined the stone terrace that stretched along the entire common area of the inn. At the center was a stone stairway down to the water.

Chance took my hand again, and we went to the stairs and started down. On the right side, close to the water's edge, was another terrace.

"In the summer there are loungers along here," he said, "and they've held weddings here."

"I bet it's a pretty venue."

"The lake is a lot prettier in the summer," he said with a chuckle.

We reached the bottom of the stairs. Ice lined the lake

from the shore, reaching several feet out before changing to open water.

"I didn't know the lake was so big," I said. The opposite shore was far away, only visible because of lights shining here and there.

"There's a cove beyond those trees," he said, pointing to the left, "and then an older lake community." He pointed to the southeast. "In that direction is a relatively new vacation rental development. Over there"—he indicated the area to our right—"is the Marks Hotel and newer homes. That's the town of Dragonfly Lake in all its glory."

The town looked sleepy and peaceful from here.

There were trees everywhere, and dark hills barely visible in the distance. The air smelled of pine and freshness. An unexplainable serenity came over me as I took it all in.

"It's beautiful," I said quietly.

Chance put his arm around my waist and pulled me into his side.

"You must be freezing," I said.

He let out a sexy, quiet laugh. "I'm fine. Though I wouldn't be opposed to having a princess warm me up."

I laughed at his reference to my costume again. "Confession: I'm anything *but* a princess in real life." I turned to face him. "But I might be convinced to help you warm up."

He brushed my hair back from my face, his gaze dipping to my lips. I moved my body into his to let him know I was on board. My heart thundered as he leaned toward me, and then his lips were on mine. A thrill shot through me at the first contact. I lifted my hands and ran them through his thick hair, pulling him closer into me.

Kissing this near stranger should seem odd, foreign, dangerous, but Chance felt natural and irresistible.

As he plunged his tongue into my mouth, I felt it to my core. I realized I might be open to more than a kiss from him. It'd been years since I'd had a fling, and I hadn't had many of them, but if this tempting man was up for it, maybe we could start the new year together. Just for a night. No strings.

Chapter Two

Chance

As a single dad of a teenage girl who broke rules more often than she followed them lately, I didn't get many evenings to myself.

On top of that, my job at the Rusty Anchor Brewing Company sometimes required working past five o'clock. I didn't mind since I liked the people, the job, and the challenge of managing the brewery's marketing efforts.

My social life was limited to early mornings at the gym and my Saturday nights with a group of dads who'd been hanging together since we were all single. Some of us weren't solo anymore. I probably always would be, at least until my daughter, Sam, was an adult and on her own. In the meantime, she was a full-time worry and then some.

I hadn't been with a woman for... Shit. I couldn't say how long it'd been since I'd gotten laid. A few hours of escape, of not needing to keep tabs on my fourteen-year-old, would be a luxury. I loved that girl with all my heart, but she'd been struggling since we moved here a year and a half ago. It got worse when she started high school last fall.

Tonight, though, it seemed things might be lining up in my favor.

Sam was spending the night at her friend Lacey's house. I'd verified with Lacey's mother that the woman would be home so the girls wouldn't be unsupervised. That translated to being able to relax at this party and have a few drinks. And maybe spend some time with the woman who'd caught my eye the second she entered the ballroom alone. Rowan.

The chemistry between us was fire, like nothing I'd ever experienced. Even before I'd gone cheesy and used my costume and boom box to get her to dance, I couldn't seem to keep my eyes from seeking her out.

She was distractingly pretty, with chestnut-brown hair that reached below her shoulders and large, captivating brown eyes. Her skin was flawless, lashes full and long, body slender and alluring even though she wore a non-revealing, narrow skirt that reached her calves, with a thick suede belt, tall boots, and a plain pink blouse for her costume.

We'd stood out in the frigid night kissing like teenagers until my balls threatened to fall off from the cold. Then we'd laughed at ourselves, made our way back up the stairs, and she'd returned my jacket before we reentered the ball-room. Once inside, she'd excused herself to go to the ladies' room.

To avoid looking like a creepy dude, in case she was giving me the blow off, I'd had to give her that space. My gaze had been on the door ever since, waiting for her to return, even as I took a ribbing from West, one of the only other singles left in the dads' group, about disappearing with my mystery woman, as he referred to her.

I was all too aware she wasn't *mine* by any stretch of the imagination. There was at least a fifty-percent chance she wouldn't reappear at the door.

She'd seemed to be as into me as I was her, but I didn't trust my judgment and sure as hell didn't trust my game where women were concerned. I suspected she was out of my league, but that didn't stop me from hoping for more time with her tonight.

The band was playing its last song of the evening, as they were packing up before midnight to let the DJ, Adrian Cormier, take over again. I didn't know him well, but I appreciated that he'd done me a solid and played along with my movie song pickup plot to win a dance with Rowan.

"I'm gonna take off," West said to the group that included Knox and Quincy, newlyweds Ben and Emerson, and me.

"Leave me as the fifth wheel," I joked. "Thanks, man."

"Your mystery woman'll be back. I saw the way she was looking at you."

"You're really leaving before midnight?" Quincy asked him.

"Need to spell my babysitter," West said, but I suspected he didn't want to be by himself at midnight, watching all the happy couples ring in a New Year of love and bliss. I couldn't blame him. I wasn't sure how long I'd stay if Rowan didn't return.

As if I'd summoned her with my thoughts, she came back into the ballroom at that moment. She paused, scanning the room. I saw the second she recognized me in the low light.

When she headed in my direction, I felt light as air. The crowd had thickened on this end of the ballroom now that the band was done playing, so I lost sight of her a few times.

Then there she was, still coming my way, her eyes on me and a shy smile on her tempting lips.

I closed the last few steps between us and took her hand as the DJ started a song.

"Hey, princess," I quipped, smiling warmly. "I was hoping you'd come back.

"I told you I would," she said.

I didn't point out that could just as easily be a blow off as a promise. "Would you like a drink? A dance?"

"I'd love some water. I'm parched."

"It's that dry, frozen air," I said, laughing again because we'd gotten so carried away out there in twenty-degree weather.

"You're lucky your arms didn't get frostbite," she said as we headed to the nearest bar.

"I'm lucky I had a beautiful girl keeping me warm."

Once we'd shared a bottle of water, we headed to the dance floor. The music was too fast for slow dancing, but I could hold my own on the upbeat songs too.

Halfway through the first song, Rowan leaned close. "You're good at this. I'm not worthy."

I laughed. "You're perfect." I pulled her closer, and we swayed together, our eyes locked, both of us grinning. I hadn't drunk more than two beers, but I was flying high because of her.

After a handful of eighties dance songs, the DJ said, "Hey, party people, the New Year's about nine minutes away. We're going to slow things down for a couple dances to get you in the mood for your New Year's kiss, so if you don't know who you'll be kissing yet, now's the time to figure it out. Don't be caught alone at the stroke of midnight!"

I didn't have the chance to question Rowan. She ran her

hands up my chest, to the back of my neck, drawing me in closer, her pretty eyes sparkling as if she'd drunk twice as many cocktails as she had. Knowing I was the cause of that sparkle sent my blood pounding through me. I ached to see what other reactions I could elicit from her, preferably with her out of that sedate costume.

That was getting ahead of myself.

"Tell me something about yourself," I said as we swayed to a Madonna slow song, trying to rein in my thoughts. I barely knew this girl and might be reading her all wrong.

She laughed quietly. "Like what?"

I shrugged. "What do you do for a living?"

A frown flitted over her face so quickly I wasn't sure I'd seen right.

"I'm a high-school teacher," she said.

"In Nashville?"

She bit her lip. "I'm between teaching positions." She averted her eyes. A couple of heartbeats later, she met my gaze again. "I had to quit my position to care for my grand-mother. She died recently of Alzheimer's."

The sadness in her eyes hit me in the gut. "I'm sorry," I said helplessly. "That must've been really hard."

She swallowed and nodded. "Let's not bring the mood down." She mustered a smile. "What about you? What do you do?"

"I'm in marketing," I said, still trying to wrap my head around what she might have gone through recently. Quitting a job to be someone's caretaker told me a lot about her character. I wanted to know more, but I didn't want to cause more sadness.

"Is this how you spent last New Year's Eve too?" She gestured to the party, then put her hand back on me where I wanted it.

"Truth? I don't remember how I spent last New Year's."

More than likely, it was something to do with my daughter. I needed to quit thinking about Sam for a few hours, but when I spent most of my waking hours worrying about her, turning that off didn't come easily.

I eased our bodies closer together and breathed in her sweet, feminine scent. "Tonight has the potential to be much more memorable," I said, watching her for a reaction.

She arched her body deeper into me and clasped her hands at my nape possessively, telling me she was feeling the pull between us too.

As the second slow song played, a server came up to us offering flutes of champagne. Rowan declined, and so did I. I'd much prefer to have my hands on her than a plastic flute.

The DJ started the countdown.

Still entwined, body to body, Rowan and I kept our eyes locked on each other as we counted along. "...four...three...two...one..."

As the crowd yelled, "Happy New Year," I fast-forwarded, taking her mouth in a too-eager kiss. The instant our mouths connected again, my whole body came alive. My blood pounded south as I ran my hands over her curves, aching to slip under her costume to feel her skin directly. There was just enough of my brain left to remember this was a dance floor in a crowded party and being too forward likely wouldn't win me any points with Rowan.

Our kiss went on as horns blew and people cheered and toasted to the New Year. This woman was more intoxicating than champagne any day.

Eventually Rowan pulled away from the kiss just enough to peer up into my eyes and ask, "Want to get out of here?"

Chapter Three

Rowan

I stopped breathing as I waited for Chance's reply.

I wasn't usually an aggressive girl. I hadn't ever initiated a hookup, not even before Christian. But the past two years had taught me how precious every moment could be. Being passive wasn't an option tonight. Not when I wanted to *feel* so badly. I wanted to feel what this man could do to me with every sensuous nerve in my body. *This* specific man.

"Hell yes," he said with a half laugh. "Let's go."

He took my hand and headed toward the door, carving a path through the crowd with me following in his wake. I loved the feel of his hand around mine: large, strong, and sure.

We finally made it through the throngs of celebrating people to the door. There were a few others leaving too. He led me to a corner, out of the way, then faced me, our hands still laced together.

"Where to?" he asked.

"My room?"

"I was hoping you'd say that."

"This way." I tugged him toward the west wing of the inn.

The hallway was relatively quiet, the roar of the party barely audible. The lights were brighter out here, seeming harsh after the dimness of the ballroom.

At the door to my room, I stopped and reached into my bra for my ID case that held my key as well. I'd left my phone in the room to further get away from the real world for a few hours. There was no longer anyone who'd need to talk to me anyway.

Once we were in my room, I closed the door, then turned as Chance advanced, gently pressing my back against the door.

The lights were off, but I could make him out by the illumination coming in under the door. Just enough to see the intent look in his eyes as he closed the distance between our mouths again. When his lips touched mine, it was urgent, passionate, unrestrained. He laced both of our hands together and framed my head with them against the door as his hard body pressed into mine, arousing a pulsing ache deep inside of me.

"I want to strip you down and kiss you everywhere," he said into my ear.

"I want you inside me," I countered, the need in me climbing, emboldening me, making me grind against him.

"That can be arranged," he said, grinning, his voice low and sexy.

I'd never been so turned on by a man's voice, never mind his kisses and his rock-solid body.

We continued to kiss, our tongues dancing, teeth knocking together, shaky breaths mingling, coming out in gasps and pants. I loosened my hands from his so I could touch him, pushing his coat off his shoulders.

"You forgot your radio," I said as he shrugged out of the coat and tossed it aside.

"Don't care," he growled as he kissed me again.

I ran my hands under his T-shirt, up his tight abs, to his solid chest, liking everything I felt. He was solid and muscular but not so much so it was intimidating. As if he went to the gym when he had time but didn't obsess about it. I kneaded his pecs, trailed my fingers to his shoulders, pulling the shirt up.

He broke off from kissing me long enough to reach to his back and yank his shirt off, then tossed it to the floor too. I untied the annoying scarf around my neck and got rid of it just as he pulled the hem of my blouse out from my skirt. I helped him get it off me.

Chance's gaze dropped to my light yellow plain-Jane bra. I'd had no thoughts of picking up a guy and bringing him to my room when I'd put it and the nonmatching pink bikini panties on. I didn't really own anything sexy anymore anyway.

He didn't seem to mind. He lowered his head and took the tip of my breast, bra and all, into his mouth as if he couldn't wait long enough to get the bra off me.

I could feel the wet heat of his mouth through the thin fabric, but I wanted more of it. I reached behind me and flicked the clasp open, then let it slide down my arms, freeing the breast Chance was still suckling. He groaned and ran his tongue over my bare nipple, letting the lingerie fall to the floor.

His mouth had everything deep inside me contracting with hot, throbbing need. I arched into him, but it didn't relieve anything. Too many clothes in the way. I went to work on his pants, unbuttoning them, unzipping, dipping my fingers inside to find him rock hard and jutting out of his underwear. He released my nipple, his head falling back.

I ran my fingers over his velvet-soft tip, eliciting another groan from him. Impatiently, needfully, I shoved his pants and boxer briefs down his thighs and wrapped my hand around his dick.

"Mmm," I growled at the feel of his thickness in my hand. I stroked him, hoping to make his need as urgent as mine.

"Jesus, that feels incredible, Rowan."

"Good," I said with a smile, loving his reaction, particularly since I was so out of practice.

"It's been a while." He sucked my nipple into his mouth again, toying with the tip, drawing a gasp of pleasure from me.

"For me too," I said on an exhale. "I don't normally—" He plucked at my other nipple with his thumb and forefinger, the ecstasy of it cutting off my words. "I don't usually do this."

"I'm so fucking glad you are tonight."

I was too, wholeheartedly. Whole-bodily. Every cell was screaming for him to fill me, to end the pulsing ache at my core.

"Right guy, right time," I said, then caught my breath again as he worked magic on both of my nipples at the same time. I let go of him so I could undo my belt and get my skirt off as fast as humanly possible, which, with the things he was doing to my body, wasn't fast enough.

As soon as he realized what I was doing, he helped. Within seconds, I was naked. He got rid of his shoes and pants, then pressed me up against the door with his body again, allowing me to feel every solid, bare inch of him against my skin.

He kissed a trail from my lips, down my chest, across both of my breasts, and lower. After circling my navel once, he went to his knees and trailed his tongue lower still, lifting one of my legs to his shoulder. When his mouth reached my center, I sucked in my breath, my legs going weak from the instant pleasure.

With one large hand supporting me at the hip, he used his other one, along with his mouth, to make me come in record time. I gripped his shoulders as my body contracted, calling out his name with a mix of incoherent words. He laved at me until I couldn't take the sensations anymore and buckled forward into him.

He stood and scooped me up, then carried me to the bed. As I lay in the near dark, trying to get my bearings back, I heard him walk over to the door. He wasn't leaving, was he?

Before I could ask, he returned. He crawled over me, supporting his weight with his arms, and found my mouth with his.

I felt his erection against my belly and clumsily reached for it, still catching my breath after he'd shot me to the stars. Chance caught my hand and angled himself to the side, resting his hip on the mattress.

When I heard the tearing of a condom packet, I understood what was going on.

"Good thinking," I said, grinning.

I appreciated that one of us had our brain at least partially intact.

"I only have one, so we better make it good," he said.

"Mmm, it's going to be good."

"No pressure, huh?" he said, smiling as he positioned

himself over me again, teasing me with his erection brushing over my belly and lower.

The bar was ridiculously low, but I didn't tell him that. He was already blowing my ever-loving mind.

He trailed kisses and nibbles along my jawline, taking his sweet time, even as he teased my center with his dick. Though it'd been less than five minutes since he'd given me an orgasm, my body responded electrically to every touch.

I grasped his sheathed length as best I could manage with him on top of me and guided him to my opening. He might think I needed time for my body to be ready again, but I was right there with him, aching to have him inside me.

When I angled my hips just right, he got the message and entered me. I let out a gasp at the feel of him, the size of him.

"Okay?" he asked, sounding like he was struggling to hold himself in check.

"More than." I wrapped my legs around him and kissed him.

"You feel so fucking amazing. I hope I can last long enough to make it good for you."

I let out a little laugh. "News flash. Already good. Stop worrying."

He kissed me thoroughly, passionately, as he thrust deliciously into me, over and over. If it was good before, he upped it to stupendous.

This man absolutely knew how to work magic on my body. Even though I'd just met him, the connection between us felt sacred. I wanted to hold on to it for hours. At the same time, I felt myself climbing higher and needing desperately to burst over the edge.

My mind shut down, and I merely held on. I hadn't felt so alive for years.

We moved as one, as if we'd been doing this together for ages. When he reached between us and brushed a finger over my clit, everything in me tightened. Another few touches from him and I exploded, clinging to him for everything I was worth. The contractions went on, wringing me out as if I was being pulled through a portal to an amazing dimension of sheer ecstasy.

"Oh, God," Chance said as he thrust his hips harder into me.

All I could do was hold on and try to breathe as he came as hard as I had.

We lay there, entwined, hearts thundering, breaths coming hard, but otherwise not moving for a spellbinding few seconds, or maybe minutes. I didn't know. Time stopped making sense.

Eventually he rolled to his side and pulled me with him. I loved the feel of his arm banding around me, his thigh against mine, his overheated, solid body all along mine. I closed my eyes and relished the bliss that was still sparkling through my body. Taking in a slow, lung-filling breath, I reveled in the luxury of being *with* someone. Not alone. I'd been alone for so very long.

"Happy New Year," he said in a low voice, his smile audible.

"Happiest," I said, falling into a deep, sated relaxation after that incredible release.

"Can't be a bad year when we start it off like that, can it?"

I shook my head, grinning as I burrowed against his chest.

Chance kissed my forehead. "I'll be right back."

"I'll be right here," I said drowsily, content that he planned to rejoin me.

This was a one-time thing, but that didn't mean we couldn't take comfort in each other for a few more hours. Though I'd never been big on cuddling, being in this man's arms was reassuring. Life-affirming. The sex had been off the charts, and lying here with him afterward, in the dark, in the quiet, listening to his breath, calmed something in my soul.

Chance

I felt my way to the bathroom, where there was a thumb-nail-sized night-light giving out just enough light to find the toilet, the sink, and the trash. I got rid of the condom and washed my hands.

Outside the bathroom, I spotted my coat. I picked it up and grabbed my phone from the pocket to check the time. It was just after one.

I hurried to the bed with my phone, setting it on the nightstand. The air was cool, particularly because of the sheen of sweat I'd worked up.

Rowan had pulled the covers back and crawled under them, since we hadn't bothered to do that earlier. She held them up now in invitation.

Was it weird to come back to bed with a woman I didn't really know? It'd been so long since I'd done this, I wasn't sure what the protocol was.

Fuck it. I wanted more time with her. Just a couple more hours. This was my rare chance to appreciate a woman's touch, her softness, her warmth. I'd been aware as hell I was overdue for a good screw, but I hadn't realized how much I'd missed being so physically close to another human.

This one night would have to tide me over for who knew how long. In a few hours, it was back to my usual overfull life and the responsibilities that took up all my headspace.

I climbed into the bed and rolled close to Rowan, pulling her naked body into mine. She made a drowsy, satisfied sound as she nestled into me. I breathed in her scent, knowing the floral sweetness was already imprinted in my memory.

Tonight had been magical, our temporary connection a rare gift. With her being from Nashville, it was clear from the start this was only for a night. Maybe that made the fireworks between us all the more spectacular. There was no pressure for more. No worries about how we'd act tomorrow. We didn't have a tomorrow. It was now or never, and we'd both chosen now.

Her breathing evened out as she sank into sleep. I was struck by how good it felt to know she trusted me enough to let down her walls, bare her body and maybe parts of her soul to me, and fall asleep in my arms.

Did I want more of this someday? Most days I couldn't even think about it, but now, with this woman curled up against me, I could admit that, yes, someday I hoped to find love again. A partner. Someday later, when Sam was an adult.

Thoughts of my daughter awakened old habits, and I loosened my hold on Rowan enough to roll to my back and pick up my phone. Just to make sure Sam was still at Lacey's.

I opened the app that showed me where her phone was, expecting the symbol to still be on Oriole Street.

Fuck.

My daughter's phone was at home, which meant *she* was at home.

I needed to get there right fucking now, not only to set a good example for her—yeah, that ship might've sailed about an hour ago—but to make sure she was okay...and alone.

Fuck, fuck, fuck.

I studied Rowan's pretty face, considering my next move. I could wake her, but I suspected she'd been through a hell storm recently. She was here at the inn to escape. She didn't have a clue I had a teenage daughter. There was no reason for her to know that. No reason to wake her with my problems. After tonight, she'd be out of my life.

When I was certain she was still asleep, I slipped out of bed, dressed as quietly and quickly as possible, and crept out of her room.

Chapter Four

Rowan

On my second full day in Dragonfly Lake, I emerged from my room a few minutes before I needed to leave for my meeting with Chloe Henry.

Yesterday I'd discovered the complementary muffins served in the inn's common area were worth getting up for.

As I walked down the hall toward the lobby, the sweet aroma of baked goods hit my nose. A girl could easily get spoiled with fresh-baked breakfast every day.

"Don't get too used to it," I muttered under my breath.

My funds were severely limited. If I thought too hard about my financial situation, I could bring on a good panic attack. I was getting a slight discount on my room at the inn by paying for a full week, but the truth was, I didn't know how many weeks I could stay here. I was on the brink of having to sleep in my car.

Once I'd quit my teaching job because my grandmother was no longer safe by herself, the two of us had ended up living on her social security income alone. There hadn't been much left after paying the rent on her two-bedroom house.

All I had left to my name were my car, my few belongings, and the proceeds of selling everything she'd owned. She'd sold her car a few years ago. The furniture and decor items hadn't netted much, but between jewelry my grandfather had given her over the years and his treasured vintage motorcycle that had still sat, unused for years, in the garage, I had a few thousand dollars to live on until I could secure a paycheck. It'd killed me a little to have to give up all but one piece of her jewelry, but I couldn't let sentiment win over practicality.

Please let Chloe Henry be an answer to my immediate money problems.

"Good morning," I said to Sadie, the girl behind the check-in desk who I'd met yesterday. I flashed her an attempt at a smile.

"Good morning, Rowan. Today's muffin offerings are blueberry and chocolate chip."

"Oh, hard choice," I said.

"You can always get one of each."

I laughed, feeling myself lighten up a little. "It's good to have options."

"Enjoy," she said as I went into the adjoining room, which was like a giant, homey living room with a big stone fireplace, several large, comfortable sofas and armchairs, and a wall of windows with a view of the wintery but beautiful lake.

Next to the living room was a dining area with a scattering of tables. There was a kitchen attached to it, with a serving counter. That's where the muffins were lined up, alongside a coffeemaker and hot tea setup.

I grabbed a chocolate chip muffin and a cup of coffee. I mixed in a packet of sweetener, then took my breakfast with me, back through the small lobby toward the door to the parking lot.

"Have a good morning," Sadie said as I went by.

"Thanks. You too."

If Chloe could offer me a job on the spot, I'd consider it a damn good morning.

Outside, the sun shone brightly, but the air was crisp. I hurried to my car and got the heater going while I stirred my coffee and took a bite of muffin. It was every bit as good as yesterday's apple cinnamon.

I headed to the Rusty Anchor Brewing Company, which was about a mile or so down Honeysuckle Road. I'd passed it yesterday when I'd gone into town to buy a few grocery items at the Country Market.

The town, I had to admit, was adorable. Though it was small, there was nothing sleepy about it. Most of the stores had been closed for New Year's Day yesterday, but I'd parked my car on the square and walked a slow lap around it, taking everything in. Lots of people had been out and about, coming and going from the bars and restaurants that were open, as well as the gym. I'd seen multiple shops I'd love to explore, even though I couldn't buy anything that wasn't a necessity.

The brewery shared a parking lot with Henry's Restaurant. When I turned into it, there were only a few cars. It wasn't quite ten a.m., so I was guessing the restaurant wasn't open yet, and Chloe had told me the brewery was closed the rest of the week for the holidays, giving its employees time off. I was grateful she'd insisted on meeting me today in spite of that.

I entered the brewery and took it in with a sweeping

look. The decor was a combination of homey wood and industrial metals, tastefully combined. Through a wall of windows on the far side were several giant gleaming metal vats where the beer was made.

In one corner stretched a long, L-shaped bar for tastings, and on the wall behind it was a sign with the Rusty Anchor logo that said, "Facilitating bad decisions since 2021," making me smile and think this might be the kind of laid-back place I needed while I healed emotionally and got back up to speed.

There were high-top tables scattered around the perimeter of the room, leaving the center as a large, open space.

"Hello?" I called out when I heard footsteps echoing.

A woman who looked to be in her thirties appeared from a hallway on the other side of the room.

"Are you Rowan?" she asked.

"I am." I walked to meet her halfway.

She had dark, glossy hair, a welcoming smile, and an air of confidence about her. She was dressed in charcoal tailored pants and a slate-blue long-sleeve polo with a Rusty Anchor logo on the chest.

"I'm Chloe. It's nice to meet you," she said warmly as we shook hands.

"You too. Thank you for meeting me on your day off."

Chloe laughed. "I'm kind of bad about taking days off sometimes, but I love my job."

"This place is impressive," I said, meaning it.

"My husband and our brewmaster and co-owner had a dream. I came along for the ride." She glowed with obvious pride. "Can I get you something to drink while we talk?"

"I'm good. I just had some coffee."

"I thought we could sit upstairs. It's a little more comfortable and warmer."

"Sure." I was interested in seeing the rest of the building and getting a better feel for everything.

I followed her back in the direction she'd come from.

"This is where we make the beer, obviously," she said, gesturing toward the towering silver vats through the windows. "Kemp Essex is our brewmaster and my husband Holden's best friend. His office is tucked inside the brew-house." Once we turned a corner, she continued, "Holden's the general manager, and his office is here."

We entered a stairwell and went up a floor.

"Up here we have the rest of the offices and another public room," Chloe continued.

"Do you function as a bar too?" I asked as we entered that public room, which had more tables and a railing that overlooked the two-story brewing room below.

"Not exactly. In the summer, we open the beer patio nightly, and we serve beer there. We have an agreement with Henry's Restaurant, which my husband also owns with his brothers, to offer a limited menu along with our beer, and the servers are technically employed by the restaurant. But as for an indoor, year-round bar, we don't do that. Not yet, anyway, and I don't think that's in the plans. We're just delving into special events."

"Like wedding receptions and parties?" I asked as we sat on stools at one of the tables, thinking this space would be ideal for both.

"Exactly. We've held events for our own business, and they worked out well. But we're still relatively new, so expanding is gradual."

"This place would make a gorgeous site for just about anything."

"I'm personally excited about the potential. I love new challenges." Chloe straightened and seemed to click into business mode. "So Presley told me a little about you and your situation. I'm so sorry about your grandmother's passing."

"Thank you. I miss her like crazy, but with Alzheimer's, there's this whole aspect of relief that she isn't suffering anymore. No one should have to go through such a horrible disease." I swallowed hard at the emotions that welled up, then attempted a bittersweet smile.

"I can't imagine what either of you went through. Presley said you're planning to search for teaching jobs for the fall eventually, but you're in need of income right away?"

I nodded. "I'll be frank with you. I never planned to quit teaching, but my grandmother couldn't afford a care-taker and wasn't safe alone. I had to choose between making money and taking care of her full-time. Through some of my education connections, I tried writing science curriculum at home, but that work wasn't steady, and it became too much for me to handle deadlines as my grand-mother required more of my time." I shook my head and shut out the emotions, wanting to paint the rest of the picture briefly so we could move on.

"I'd make the same decision again if I had to do it over," I continued, "but it's put me in a dire financial situation. We were living on her social security, and of course that ended when she died. I considered substitute teaching, but I really need something a little more predictable."

"Substituting would be a challenge," Chloe said. "Even if you could get a position each day, I shudder to think of facing a classroom of kids. Of course, I'm not cut out to be any kind of teacher." She smiled. "Teachers are special souls, for sure. I have the utmost respect for them. For you."

"Thanks," I said. "It's definitely not for everybody, but I did it for three years and loved the kids. I do want to eventually get back to it, but I need some time before I walk back into a classroom full of teenagers. I'm flexible and a fast learner. I'm reliable and get along with all kinds of personalities. If you have any positions available, I'm all ears."

"I'm looking for an assistant for Holden and me," she said, watching me closely. "We've grown to the point where our small staff is stretched to the limit. We need a detail person. Particularly as we begin marketing our venue for events. As much as I'd love to have my hand in everything, there are only so many hours in a day, and we have a one-year-old at home."

Since I hadn't known much about Chloe's business before, I'd figured I would be involved in serving or bartending or something similar. This sounded even better.

"I'm intrigued," I said.

She told me more about what she envisioned me doing on a daily basis. It would be a wide-range, kind of do-whatever's-needed position, as it was new, and she was still figuring it out. She was apologetic for the lack of structure.

I was fine with it and relieved as hell she might be willing to hire me in spite of my plans to return to teaching. I could put up with a lot to have a full-time paycheck right away.

"What questions do you have for me?" she asked.

I laughed. "What can I do to convince you to hire me? I love the atmosphere here, and you seem like you'd be wonderful to work with."

"I like to think I'm nicer than a classroom full of teenagers," she said. "Most days. We're a baby company, but

Holden and Kemp really know what they're doing. Thanks to our ties to the restaurant, which already had a sterling reputation, we've been getting regional attention almost from the start, so we're growing fast. One of the challenges of growth is the pace of hiring additional employees. We've needed an assistant for months but dragged our feet. Then Presley called."

"Presley's amazing," I said of the girl who'd lived next door to me for half of my childhood. We'd reconnected at my grandmother's funeral and met for lunch a few days later. If Chloe hired me, I didn't know how I'd ever pay Presley back for the connection.

"She's the best. Like the sister I never had," Chloe said. "She vouched for you completely, but even if she hadn't, I like you and suspect we'll work very well together. That's a lot more important to me in this position than your specific skill set."

I asked her about work hours, and then before I could inquire about money, she spelled out the salary and benefits, which mostly kicked in after six months. I wasn't too concerned about paid vacation, but the health insurance would be welcome. I'd had to drop mine months ago because I couldn't afford the premiums.

"Everything sounds great," I said. "I'd love the opportunity."

"Can you start on Monday?"

"Absolutely." I sat up straighter, hope pumping through me.

"Then I'll see you then. Eight a.m."

"I'm hired?"

Chloe held out her hand for me to shake. "Welcome aboard, Rowan."

Chapter Five

Rowan

My wardrobe had two settings: teacher and not-leaving-the-house.

I wasn't sure what brewery-appropriate outfits consisted of, but for my first day at my new job, I'd decided on a multicolored knit blouse under a cropped blazer with stone-gray slacks. I paired it all with suede booties with chunky heels. It was comfortable but professional and lent me a little confidence as I embarked on this job I had zero experience doing and almost as few ideas about what to expect.

I liked Chloe though, and I trusted Presley. If she thought I could work with her bestie, then I likely could. I hoped the rest of the brewery employees were easy to work with too.

Oh, who was I kidding? I just needed to do whatever was necessary to earn a paycheck. If I ended up enjoying the job, it would be a bonus.

I arrived twenty minutes early. Chloe was there, and I

met her husband, Holden. The two of them were impossible not to like.

My first hour plus was spent filling out paperwork and going over HR stuff with Holden.

"Ready for a tour?" Chloe said when I returned to her office.

"I'd love it." I didn't know the first thing about how beer was brewed, but as a science geek at heart, I couldn't wait to learn more about the process.

Chloe stood and came around her desk. "Everything go okay with paperwork?"

"Easy-peasy, except the part about a permanent address. Holden said to use the inn's address for now and change it when I figure out where I'm going next."

"I hope you can find something soon. The inn is cozy and comfortable, but I imagine you'd like to get settled."

"I've been fantasizing about having a full-size fridge," I joked. "Being able to make my own meals will help cut down on expenses."

"For sure. Which reminds me, lunch is on us today."

"Oh, I didn't mean—"

"It was already planned," Chloe insisted. "Holden and I are treating you to Henry's. Have you eaten there before?"

I shook my head. "I can't wait though. I've heard good things about it."

"I might be biased, considering it has my married name on the sign, but I think you'll love it. Cash, my brother-in-law, is a truly talented chef."

"At the risk of sounding like a grade-schooler, I can't wait for lunch," I said.

We headed down the hall, past the closed doors of the other offices, to the stairway. On the main floor, I followed

Chloe to what she called the brewhouse—the cavernous two-story room with the silver vats.

I met one of the assistant brewers, Gianna. I listened raptly as Chloe explained the brewing process step by step, with Gianna throwing in details along the way.

"This makes my chemistry-loving heart happy," I told them.

"If nothing else, you'll have new material to take to your next teaching job," Chloe said.

"Do you offer tours to the public?" I asked.

"We do on weekends. Right now we don't have a dedicated tour guide, so several of us alternate. Someday soon we'll expand. Our tastings at the end are popular and help us sell beer."

"Have you tasted any of our brews yet?" Gianna asked.

"Not yet," I admitted.

"Today at lunch we'll do a flight so you know what we're selling. If you like beer?"

I laughed. "I like beer. Shouldn't that be a prerequisite for being hired?"

"Failure on my part," Chloe said, grinning as she led me out of the brewhouse.

She showed me through the main-floor public room, with the tasting counter and the minikitchen for events. We stopped at the loading dock and took a brief look into the storage area. Then I followed her up the stairs again as she explained her vision for special events. Both floors would be available, as well as the beer patio, which she pointed out through the second-floor windows, in the summer.

"If we use all three, we have a capacity of three hundred guests," Chloe explained. "Henry's adds catering options. You can't beat the view in the spring, summer, and fall."

"I can picture some beautiful events, even inside in the winter. The atmosphere is homey but classy."

"That's exactly what we were going for. Come this way, and I'll show you your office."

"I get an office?" I asked.

"We have one empty one. You might have to share it at times, and you'll spend a lot of time in mine, but you're welcome to personalize it however you want, within reason." She pointed to one of the closed doors. "That's Mateo's office. He's on the road more often than he's here, but you'll meet him soon. He's our director of sales and distribution."

"So he gets Rusty Anchor into restaurants and bars?"

"That's right. He's very good at what he does. We're lucky to have him." She took out a key chain and unlocked the office on the inside corner. "This is you."

There was a desk with a computer on it and a table with four chairs but not much else. No windows, but the overhead lights were warm and daylight bright with a dimmer switch.

"It's everything I'll need," I said. I didn't imagine I'd do much to decorate it. I didn't have many photos or posters to put on the walls.

"Sorry it's so bland." Chloe frowned at it as if she was seeing it for the first time. "It needs colorful paintings. If you don't have anything you want to bring, you and I can pick some out, and we'll order them."

"That sounds great. I don't think my high-school science classroom materials would've fit in."

She left the door open and led me back toward her office, but she paused at the open door that had previously been closed. "Come meet our director of marketing," she said, peering into the office with a smile.

I followed her. When I laid eyes on the man rising behind the desk, it was all I could do to keep moving forward.

No. Fucking. Way.

"Chance Cordova, this is Rowan Andrews, our new assistant."

I felt like I moved in slow motion toward the desk, taking in the so-damn-handsome face of the man I'd ushered in the New Year with. Meeting his gaze, I watched for a glint of recognition from him, but he gave no hint that we'd ever met.

Holy awkward moment.

My heart thundered in my chest as I tried to figure out how to handle this, deciding in a flash to follow his lead.

"Pleased to meet you," he said as he shook my hand with a firm grip and a benign smile.

"Hello," I managed, my mouth going dry. I couldn't get out any pleasantries about how nice it was to "meet" him.

"Welcome to Rusty Anchor." His eyes were still on me, telling me he did indeed recognize me—my God, I'd hope he would recognize me—but he'd decided not to reveal our connection.

Okay then.

"Thank you," I said formally. "I'm looking forward to the challenge."

I only half listened as Chloe told him this was an experiment for both of us, with me planning to return to teaching in the fall and her getting a better idea of how she could best use an assistant. I was too lost in my head.

I need this job. I can't do anything to screw it up.

Would it really screw it up if Chloe knew I'd met Chance a few nights ago?

I couldn't make sense of why he was pretending not to

know me unless he was embarrassed or regretful. Maybe he was. He *had* sneaked out while I was asleep.

I'd been neither...until now.

"Holden and I are taking Rowan to Henry's for lunch," Chloe said, apparently not noticing any weirdness between him and me. Which was good. "We'd love to have you join us."

"I have an errand I have to run over lunch," Chance said, his eyes on Chloe now. "I'll have to pass today."

An errand or he didn't want to have lunch with me?

Hello, complex. I was suddenly developing one.

"Next time," Chloe said. "We have lots to cover, so we'll let you get back to work."

"Have a good first day," he said to me with a smile. That dimpled smile.

Flustered, I managed to get out, "Thanks. I hope to," then walked out after Chloe, internally flipping out.

Chapter Six

Chance

What a fucking day.

By the time my meeting at Henry's Restaurant with Seth Henry and Kennedy Clayborne, the woman who handled the restaurant's social media, was over, it was going on six p.m., and Rowan had left the brewery for the day.

Rowan. Our newest employee.

What were the chances the one hookup I'd had in more than two years turned out to be Rusty Anchor's new hire? She was one of only eight people who worked here, including myself. There'd be no avoiding frequent, close contact with Rowan Andrews.

Compounding the problem was that, when she'd walked into my office this morning, I'd been just as attracted to her then as when I'd laid eyes on her New Year's Eve. I could deny it all I wanted, but our night together hadn't cooled the fire or gotten a damn thing out of my system.

I'd been shocked when she'd suddenly been standing in my office, and then what had I done?

Acted like I'd never seen her before.

Talk about a douchebag move.

It hadn't been a conscious decision so much as a reaction. A guilty reaction, probably, though what did I have to feel guilty about? Our night together—okay, our *few hours* together—had been mutual, consensual, and pretty fucking amazing.

Sure, and then I ran away when I thought Sam was causing trouble.

Which was legit, but in hindsight, it probably hadn't won me any points with Rowan.

Now that we were coworkers, I'd prefer if she didn't have a bad opinion of me.

I made my way from Henry's to the brewery to shut down for the day and grab my coat. The weather had turned nasty over the past few hours, with a freezing rain coming down. That wasn't enough to prevent me from heading out to the Honeysuckle Inn. I owed Rowan an apology.

Back in my office, I slid my laptop into my bag, put my coat on, and headed out, saluting Kemp in the brewhouse as I went by.

Before taking off toward the inn, I checked my daughter's location yet again. On the one hand, I didn't like monitoring her so closely. On the other, more times than not, I discovered her not where she was supposed to be.

This time she was still in the right place, at our house. I had no way of knowing whether she was breaking any of our rules by having friends over when I wasn't home, but for now I had to give her the benefit of the doubt. There was a fine line between micromanaging a teenager and developing a mutual trust that could still somehow keep her safe. I had yet to master where the fuck that line was, but it wasn't for lack of trying.

Only when I'd parked in the inn's lot did I stop to wonder how a surprise visit to Rowan would go over. I didn't have other options though. I'd had every intention to get her alone for a few minutes at work, but she'd been shadowing Chloe every time I'd seen her in between my meetings and phone calls.

I didn't have her phone number, so I didn't know any other way to initiate a private conversation.

Without further waffling, I got out of my SUV, put my head down against the driving wind and sleet, and headed inside. I spared the guy at the front desk a quick glance and a friendly smile, relieved it wasn't Ava or Anna, both of whom I knew well. They'd want to know what I was doing here. I preferred to keep my ties to Rowan private. It was nobody's business but ours.

Outside her door, I paused, preparing myself to see her again. Then I knocked.

There was a peephole, and I could hear her using it, so when she opened the door, I was momentarily relieved.

"Hi," I said. I offered a smile, part conciliatory and part an involuntary reaction to seeing her again.

"Chance," she greeted, not smiling. "What are you doing here?"

"I didn't know how else to contact you. I wanted to clear some things up. Can I come in?"

She glanced both ways, as if she too had thoughts of keeping our connection private. There was no one else in the hall.

Rowan opened the door farther and let me in. I took in the room for the first time with the lights on. It was a pretty average hotel room with an armchair, a desk, a TV on a long cabinet with drawers and a minifridge, and the bed. Just a glance at the bed had my memories flaring and my body going hot.

I did my best to shove those thoughts aside.

It appeared she'd been sitting on top of the made bed, reading a book, and eating a sandwich.

"Sorry to interrupt your dinner," I said.

She shrugged and looked a little embarrassed. "It's just PB and J."

She stood at the foot of the bed, watching me expectantly. She'd changed from what she'd worn to work today into flared yoga pants with a purple-and-lavender-swirled design and an oversized gray hoodie. Her hair was thrown up on her head in a devil-may-care way. She looked comfortable, a little rumpled, and still sexy as hell.

I opened my mouth to speak, but I hadn't planned out what to say, so I closed it again.

"I interviewed with Chloe on Friday," she said. "I swear I had no idea you worked there until today."

"I didn't even know she was looking for an assistant."

"I'm not sure she was." She bit her lower lip, eyes averted, then met my gaze. "Do you want to sit?" She gestured to the armchair.

Without speaking, I sat on the edge of it.

"I didn't think I'd see you again after New Year's Eve," she said as she lowered herself to the bed, facing my chair. "We didn't exactly tell each other our life stories."

I couldn't help a smile. "We had other things on our minds."

She made eye contact again, and there was a flash of heat in hers. "We did. And then you were gone."

"Yeah, sorry to sneak out. I'd had every intention of staying longer but..."

Hell. This was suddenly awkward. She had no idea I was a dad. A dad of a rule-breaking teenager who didn't seem to like me, no less. Good thing I wasn't trying to impress her or get in her bed again, because my situation was sure to put any single woman off. Particularly a younger one like Rowan.

"It's okay," she said before I could explain more. "It was a one-night thing. I never had any ideas other than that."

"It was." Whether we'd said as much in words was beside the point. As far as I'd known, she was just in town for a few days. "I have a fourteen-year-old daughter."

Her attention shot to my face, her brows dipping. "Are you married?"

"No. My wife died when Sam was six."

Her demeanor shifted to sympathy. "I'm sorry, Chance."

"My daughter... She's had a hard time since we moved here. Well, since before that, but she's still trying to fit in..." I shook my head. She didn't need to know all the details. "Anyway, she was staying at a friend's house New Year's Eve. I made sure the girl's mother was home. Everything should've been fine. I figured it was one night I could relax and have a good time, but I happened to check her phone location when you fell asleep, and she was back at our house."

"Oh." She frowned. "That's...not good? It was, like, after one in the morning."

"Right." I shook my head, hurting once again for my little girl who wasn't so little anymore. "When I got home, I found out her friend deserted her for a boy, so she came home. Physically safe but totally upset."

"Understandable. I'm glad you were there for her."

"Yeah. She wasn't, unfortunately. Glad I was there, I mean." These days it seemed like she hated me more often than not. "So...that's the story of why I left abruptly."

"It's okay. You owed me nothing. In a way you did us both a favor because we avoided an awkward morning after."

"Until today, huh? Delayed awkward moment."

"I was shocked, but then you made it awkward," she said.

"I'm sorry. I fucked up. I don't know why I pretended we'd never met other than I was stunned to see you in my office. It was a knee-jerk decision, and it was the wrong one."

"Apology accepted. I'm fine with being a shameful secret from your recent past." Her lips hinted at a grin.

"Not shameful at all, but I hope we can keep it in the past and handle being just coworkers. I've got a lot going on with my kid and no room for entanglements."

Rowan smiled a little fuller, but it was tinged with melancholy. "Believe me, I'm not in any mental space where I'm up for entanglements either."

"Your grandmother," I said, nodding. "You said you were getting away. I thought you meant for a week or something."

Rowan pulled her legs up to sit crisscross, her eyes on her lap. "I lived with her in a rental house for the past few years. I moved in because she couldn't live alone safely, couldn't afford caretakers, and adamantly refused to move into a facility."

"She had Alzheimer's, right?"

She nodded. "When I moved in, I realized she was a lot worse than I thought. She did her best to hide it from me, but being there every day, it became evident. One day when I was at work, she left the house on foot and wandered off."

She closed her eyes and swallowed, and I could tell she was fighting to keep her composure.

"When I came home from work, I couldn't find her. The police put out a silver alert. They found her nearly two miles away a few hours later, sitting on a bench outside of a Dairy Queen, upset because she couldn't find her purse to pay for some ice cream."

"That's heartbreaking."

She nodded, swallowed again. "After that, I installed special dementia alarms on the doors. I hired aides to stay with her while I was gone, but she hated it. She was afraid of them and tried to get away from them. Even though some of the aides were incredibly caring and patient, she felt threatened by them and didn't understand what they were going to do to her. They were there to help her and keep her safe, but no matter how many times I reminded her of that, she forgot. When she bit one of them and drew blood, I knew I had to make changes for everyone's sake."

"So you quit your job?"

"I quit my job and took care of her."

"That's... Jesus, that must've been a lot."

She let out a sad laugh. "I didn't feel like I had a lot of options." She swiped under her eyes. "Sorry. Still raw, I guess. I just...loved her so much."

I couldn't imagine doing what she'd done. "She was incredibly lucky to have you."

"I was lucky to have her. She and my grandfather raised me from the time my parents were killed in an accident."

"How old were you when that happened?"

"Seven. They didn't blink, just moved me in and loved me." She pressed her lips together. "I couldn't let her go to a memory care facility. I'm sure there are decent ones out there, but the thought of her sitting alone in her room, not knowing where she was, being surrounded by eternal strangers because she couldn't remember meeting them from one day to the next..."

Rowan went silent, thoughtful, and I tried to figure out what to say. There were no words for what she'd been through, what she'd sacrificed. She'd obviously loved her grandmother fiercely.

She popped up off the bed and let out a self-conscious half laugh. "I'm sorry. I don't know why I told you all that. Talk about awkward."

"You're fine. You've been through hell." I had an over-powering urge to hug her, but we'd just agreed we were nothing more than coworkers going forward.

"My whole point is, when she died, I couldn't afford to keep renting the house, so I sold everything in it. A friend of mine connected me with Chloe, and here I am. She agreed to take me on, whether she was ready to hire an assistant or not."

"But you're planning to go back to teaching?"

"I'm hoping to take a position for the fall. I love teaching, but it takes a lot of energy, and I just don't have it in me right now."

"You'll get it back," I said. "I hope Dragonfly Lake helps you heal."

"Thanks."

"Are you planning to get an apartment?"

"I'll get more serious about that once I get a paycheck."

I stood, reminding myself Rowan's living situation wasn't my business. "I should let you get back to your PB and J. Thank you for telling me more about your grandmother," I said, making a point of keeping distance between us. "I'm glad Chloe was able to offer you a job."

"Me too. Someday I hope I can pay her and Presley back." She looked pensive for a moment.

"I imagine having an assistant will be payback enough for Chloe. She handles a lot."

"I've got a steep learning curve. But the brewing process? Chemistry 101. I've got that part down after my tour."

"I bet you do. I hadn't thought of it that way before." I chuckled. "If not for the fact we were making alcohol, tours would be a great opportunity for high school chemistry classes."

"If not for that fact," she repeated, grinning.

I walked to the door, and she followed me.

"I'm glad we talked," I said.

"Me too. Going forward, strictly coworkers."

Facing her, my hand on the knob, I peered down at her and got caught up in her expressive brown eyes. I had to fight not to glance at her lips, not to let myself think about kissing her.

"I'll see you at work tomorrow, coworker." I opened the door and got the hell out of there before I did something dumb.

As I went out into the crappy weather, I forced my thoughts to my daughter and pulled out my phone to make dinner plans with the only female I had room for in my life.

Chapter Seven

Rowan

After two and a half weeks at my new job, I could say with certainty this had been a good move for me.

This small town felt healing somehow. Anna, who managed the inn for Ava, claimed it was the lake, even in the winter. The scenery and the half-frozen water were soothing to gaze at from my balcony door or the inn's cozy living area. So was being able to read when I wanted to and nap when I needed to, which turned out to be embarrassingly a lot more than I'd ever napped before.

I genuinely liked working at the brewery. The atmosphere was warm and positive. Holden and Chloe were gracious and patient and appreciated having an assistant. The other employees, Chance included, seemed to enjoy what they did. After working in a tension-filled, bureaucracy-laden, big-city high school, I welcomed the intimate, low-pressure environment. I still hoped to go back to a classroom eventually because I was dedicated to education and thrived on connecting with teenagers, but this was the ideal respite while I recovered from the past few years.

Working with my one-night-stand guy?

On the surface, I was handling it okay.

No one at work knew about our fling. Chance had told me, when we both found ourselves at the coffee machine one morning, that no one else from the brewery had been at the inn's party, but everyone knew people who had been, including some of Chloe's close friends. If someone figured out our secret, we'd acknowledge it, point out it wasn't an issue, and move on.

Inside I wasn't so unbothered or indifferent. My attraction to him hadn't dimmed. Seeing his professional side, where he was intelligent, confident, and damn good at what he did, did nothing to cool the flames. I hadn't been drunk on New Year's Eve. My judgment held up in the daylight. He was, to me, the kind of guy I could fall for in a different lifetime, or maybe just a different era of this lifetime. The few times we'd been alone, my pulse raced, and my mouth went dry. My body *remembered*.

I made a point of blocking out those memories as much as possible. What I'd told him still held true. I had zero mental space for entanglements or drama. I was grieving the woman who'd raised me, as well as recovering physically and mentally from a relentlessly stressful multiyear period of caretaking. There was a reason they said people shouldn't make major decisions for a full year after a loss.

Not that Chance was a major decision. But a relationship with anyone could lead to one.

Anyway, work was good. I could ignore my attraction to my fling. I was learning my duties and so far could handle all of them.

Best of all, I'd received my first paycheck, so I could breathe—and afford an evening out like tonight.

"There she is," Chloe said as Presley made her way through the tables in Henry's Restaurant toward us.

"Hey, ladies," Presley said when she reached our table in the farthest corner of the restaurant. Even though it was off-season and a weeknight, Henry's was filled to the rafters.

Both Chloe and I stood and hugged Presley in turn.

"Hey, you," she said to me, holding on to me a little longer, conveying concern. "How are you doing?"

I nodded as I said, "I'm doing okay. At least until some kind, caring girl goes out of her way to ask me how I'm doing."

We all laughed, relieving the pressure behind my eyes, which was what I'd intended.

"My girl Chloe's treating you okay?" Presley asked as she sat across from Chloe, next to me at the table for four that looked out on the dark lake.

"Chloe's the best boss ever, and I'm not saying that to kiss up."

"Aww," Chloe said. "Dinner's on me tonight because, thanks to you two, my life is slightly smoother. Thanks for connecting us, Pres."

"You're sweet," I told Chloe, "but the whole point of tonight is for *me* to thank the two of you. Without you, I'd be sleeping in my car and working in food service, which I've proven in the past is not my strength."

"I'm thrilled it's working out," Presley said. "But you're not treating. You're saving every penny. I've got this one."

"We'll see," Chloe said, grinning.

Technically she was part owner of this place. She had connections and maybe even a sign-in to the customer billing system.

If I didn't end up paying tonight, I'd find a different way to thank them.

"So you've known each other since middle school, right?" Chloe asked.

"I was in middle school," Presley said. "Rowan was younger."

"Presley was my babysitter. I met her when I moved in with my grandparents."

"They lived next door to us," she added. "They were special people. I used to hang out with her grandmother even before Rowan came to live with them. That woman taught me how to bake cookies."

"Gram made the best chocolate chip," I said with conviction.

"That's the truth. Somehow mine were never as good, even though I followed her recipe," Presley said.

"Same," I said. "Anyway, there's six years between us, so Presley was always more like an older sister or cousin. I hadn't seen her since my college graduation party. I was so glad to see her at Gram's funeral."

"I wouldn't miss it," Presley said. "I loved that woman like she was my own grandma."

My eyes filled with tears. "Presley insisted on a lunch date so we could catch up. That's when she thought of connecting you and me."

"Genius idea, my friend," Chloe said to her bestie. As I understood it, they'd met in college and clicked.

Our server, Bria, came by and took Presley's merlot order and our dinner orders, then hurried off.

"You look fancy tonight, Pres. Did you come straight from the office?" Chloe asked.

Presley wore a cropped gray blazer over a navy blouse and tailored pants. She'd paired it all with some awe-inspiring platform stilettos I could never handle for a full workday.

"I worked from home today," Presley replied, "but I had an important thing this afternoon." Her blue eyes sparkled with excitement. "It's why I'm late."

"What kind of thing?" Chloe asked.

"I put an offer on a house." Presley clasped her hands together in front of her mouth, as if holding in her excitement.

"You're buying a *house*?" Chloe asked, leaning on the table.

"*If* the offer is accepted."

"Where is this house?" Chloe asked.

Presley leaned a little closer, her voice going quieter. "Here in Dragonfly Lake. Lakefront."

Chloe tilted her head, as if trying to figure out where that could be.

"So you're moving here?" I asked. I'd like nothing more than to get to know Presley better as an adult.

"Maybe eventually." Presley took her win from the server, then took a sip. "I might rent it out to vacationers or use it myself on weekends. But first it needs some work."

"Where's the house?" Chloe asked. "I don't pay close attention, but I know when Emerson was looking before the holidays, there was almost nothing on the market."

"Officially the listing goes live tomorrow." Presley set her glass on the table.

"How'd you manage that?" Chloe asked.

Presley's lips curved into a smile. "I've got connections."

"Stop." Chloe rolled her eyes.

"The agent might be my client," she said vaguely. "Anyway, it's not a done deal."

"When are you supposed to hear?" I asked.

"I gave them two days, but I'm hoping for sooner. It's a cash offer but lower than they're planning to ask."

"And you're keeping your job and your condo in Nashville?" Chloe asked.

"For now."

Which told me money was not a struggle for her. But then I knew she was a successful financial planner.

Chloe eyed her, assessing. "What's going on in that head of yours, Pres? You don't just randomly buy real estate without a plan."

Presley frowned. "I don't know exactly. I just have this gut feeling—and I'm not talking about the killer cramps going on today. I feel like I need to get my ducks in a row. You know I don't trust Rob Landers."

"He's a weasel," Chloe said, then filled me in. "Her insecure asshole of a boss."

"Ew," I said. "Lucky for me, my boss is awesome. That can make or break a job."

"You're so good for my ego," Chloe said, grinning.

I asked Presley, "Do you think your job's in jeopardy or something?"

She bit her lip thoughtfully. "There's no concrete reason to think that. I'm doing well for my clients—"

"What she's not saying is she's one of her company's best, month after month, year after year," Chloe interjected.

Presley continued, "Like I said, just a gut feeling."

"You don't need that job or the stress it brings," Chloe said.

"I'm starting to think you're right." Presley angled to look beyond Chloe. "Your husband and daughter are here."

Holden stood at a table of diners, chatting them up, his one-year-old daughter on his shoulders, gripping his head with both hands and giggling.

"It should be illegal to be that adorable," I said. I'd met Sutton Henry a few times at work when her parents brought her in.

"Look at that ham," Presley said.

"She loves her daddy." Chloe's wide grin said she did too.

"I meant Holden. Your hubby is ridiculously in love with her."

"He's the best dad ever," Chloe said. "And I forgot to warn you we're getting a fourth for the evening. Holden's got ping-pong league, so he's dropping Sutton off. As soon as he finishes showing her off to anyone who'll listen." She got up to get her daughter.

I knew from discussions at work Chance and Kemp were in that same ping-pong league. I shut down on the thrill that zinged through me just at the thought of my one-night guy.

"That little girl right there is my favorite kid in the world," Presley said.

"She's pretty irresistible."

"Chloe's a lucky girl," Presley said as Chloe arrived with little Sutton in her arms.

"Hey, cutie patootie," I said.

"Hi, favorite girl," Presley said.

"I need to get her a high chair," Chloe said.

"I'll take her." Presley held out her arms. "Come to Auntie Presley, Sutton."

Sutton pointed at her and said, "Guh!"

"I'll be right back." Chloe set Sutton on Presley's lap, hung the baby bag over her chair back, and went off for a high chair.

Sutton stared at me curiously, so I shot her a smile. "I'm

Rowan. I met you at your mommy and daddy's work. Your outfit is adorable."

Sutton held out both arms to me.

Presley's mouth gaped open. "You want Rowan instead of me? I'm shattered!" She winked at me as the little girl, unbothered, leaned toward me.

When I made room, Presley transferred Sutton to my lap.

"Hi, cutie pie." I pressed a kiss to the top of her head, hugged her, then handed her my spoon when she pointed at it.

"You're a natural," Presley said. "You'll make a great mom someday."

I forced my brain to skip over that comment entirely and changed the subject.

"Tell me about your house," I said.

Before she could say anything, Bria served us our entrees. My southern shrimp and grits had sounded so good when I'd ordered it, but now my stomach churned. My appetite had been wonky for months, likely due to stress. Lately it'd gotten worse rather than better though, with food bringing on a wave of nausea more often than not. It didn't make sense, but then I knew grief could mess a body up just as much as stress.

Chloe returned, and we settled Sutton in her high chair then started into our meals. I took several small bites of grits, thinking getting something in my empty stomach would calm its uneasiness.

"God, this is good," Presley said of her beer-battered walleye. "You might've married the wrong Henry brother, Chloe."

Chloe laughed. "Cash is a good chef, but Holden's my soul mate."

"When's Ava due?" I asked of Cash's wife, the inn owner who'd been so welcoming from that very first night.

"In March. She's got about six weeks left," Chloe said.

"As long as her husband doesn't stop cooking for me," Presley said, grinning. Then her expression turned to a frown. "Chlo, favor to ask. Can I sleep on your sofa tonight? I'm thinking another drink would help dull the crampiness."

"Bad periods?" I asked, able to relate to that with every fiber of my being.

"She gets horrible ones," Chloe said. "For as long as I've known her."

"I have endometriosis," Presley said as she picked up her drink.

"I do too," I said.

"It's a big bag of suckage," Presley said. "Do you have pain in between periods too?"

"Yessss. Like, eighty percent of the time." I set my fork down hard once the words were out of my mouth, struck by a realization.

"Are you okay?" Chloe asked me, watching me closely.

I glanced up at her, my mind spinning. "Yeah. I just..." I shook my head. "I just realized I haven't had that pain since I've lived here. Three weeks. That's unheard of."

"That's wonderful," Chloe said.

"It's...unusual, but I'll take it," I said.

"Any chance you could be pregnant?" Presley asked. "One of my colleagues has endo pretty bad, but when she was pregnant, the pain went away."

The bite I'd just swallowed nearly came back up. "N-no," I said automatically. I tried to remember the date, did the math. Twenty-three days since New Year's, but... "No."

I met the gazes of both women, who were watching me with concern.

"Are you sure?" Presley asked.

I picked up my napkin and nervously wiped my mouth as I considered telling them more. It'd been a while since I'd had girlfriends on a confiding level. I'd had several at my teaching job, but we'd gradually lost touch once I quit and wasn't able to meet them for happy hours or movie nights. With a slow, shaky breath, I realized how much I'd missed that kind of connection.

"My ob-gyn said my odds of ever having children are tiny unless I have a procedure," I said quietly.

"I'm sorry to hear that," Chloe said, looking genuinely upset for me.

Presley tilted her head. "There's still a chance, you know? If you were with someone…"

My insides fluttered nervously. I blurted out, "I had a fling on New Year's Eve." I could tell them that much, but no way would I reveal who I'd been with.

I could tell they were calculating the weeks.

"Totally possible," Presley said.

"But so improbable." I couldn't think straight. My brain was stuttering along, trying to imagine. In the year plus I'd been with Christian, there'd been no pregnancy scares despite us being careless with birth control.

I'd been devastated by my doctor's prognosis. I'd always wanted to have babies. When I'd pictured my future, the husband's face was blurry and unclear, but there were kids in the equation every time. Yes, I'd likely have the procedure eventually to increase my odds, but the question remained whether my body would cooperate with my dream of being a mom.

If one hundred women had the same prognosis, a handful of us could end up pregnant.

What if one of them was me?

No, surely not. It would be the worst timing ever. I'd just started adjusting to being responsible only for me after neglecting myself for so long. This was my healing phase, my refinding myself era. For me to be pregnant would be the utmost in irony ever.

That aside, if by some long-shot, miraculous act of the universe I was pregnant, the circumstances were so not ideal. A one-night stand with a man I barely knew, who apparently had his hands full with a teenage daughter and wanted nothing to do with me beyond working together. And me, a tangle of grief, soul-deep fatigue, and emotional vulnerability. In other words, a verifiable shit show.

"Do you want to take a test?" Chloe asked with so much empathy in her tone I could cry.

God. A pregnancy test. I'd never needed one before. I wasn't convinced I needed one now.

"Do you think that's premature?" I asked.

"Not if it happened New Year's Eve." Presley squeezed my wrist lightly. "It's whatever you're comfortable with, hon. But if it were me, I wouldn't be able to sleep until I knew one way or the other."

"Do you have any other symptoms?" Chloe asked.

I met her eyes as it hit me that, yes, I did. "Nausea."

Presley sucked in an audible breath.

There was almost no part of me that really thought I could be pregnant. I'd made peace with the odds, mostly, at least until I had the procedure. Or maybe I just hadn't had any bandwidth to think about it for ages. Pregnancy wasn't on my radar. This was likely something else, which led to scarier questions. What could be wrong with my body now?

Maybe that seemed pessimistic, but I'd struggled with pain for so long that it seemed a lot more logical than being pregnant.

"It's not too early to test?" I asked, understanding that ruling out pregnancy was my first step.

"Not at all," Chloe said, breaking up another of her daughter's chicken fingers into bite-sized pieces. "A little advice though... If you want to avoid gossip, I wouldn't recommend buying tests at the Country Market. People will find out fast."

Right. Because I was living and working in a small town now.

"I could go buy some," Presley said. "They can speculate all they want about me."

"No need," Chloe said. "I have at least two unused tests at home. They're yours. If you want moral support, you can test at my house. Holden's out for the evening."

I inhaled slowly, trying to settle myself down as I looked from Chloe to Presley. "If I'm not pregnant, and I honestly don't think I am, then something weird is going on. So... yeah. I'll take you up on that."

I couldn't pass up the offer of moral support and girlfriends who'd help me through, whatever the results ended up being.

Chapter Eight

Chance

Parents who joked about locking their daughter in a dungeon until she was thirty had a valid idea.

Was it a mistake or was it fortunate that I'd checked Sam's location on my phone between the second and third games of ping-pong and discovered she was at the beach? In the dark? In late January? Temperature in the low thirties?

Her safety was paramount, so I supposed it was a lucky catch, but as I left Kemp, my table tennis partner, hanging with one game left, I was just about ready to throw my hands up and tell her to do whatever the hell she wanted since she clearly had no intention of following my rules.

"I'm sorry, man," I said to Kemp after breaking the news to him.

He brushed it off with a shake of his head and a wave. "Dude, don't think twice about it. Go get your daughter."

"You really think it's illegal to lock them in their room?"

He laughed. "Get out of here. Good luck."

A shit ton of luck was what I'd need to get my daughter through her teen years unscathed. Doing it without her hating me would be nothing short of a miracle.

I walked out of the community center into the cold evening, biting down on the urge to punch walls on the way.

Sam had always been a daddy's girl, even before her mother had died. When she'd turned eleven, everything had changed, almost overnight. She growled at me, was embarrassed by me, shut down on me, yet still sometimes hugged me and told me she loved me. Puberty was like that, or so all the parenting websites and books said, but what they couldn't tell me was how the hell to navigate it. I'd been over my head for three years and counting. Or really more like fourteen.

I got into my SUV and headed the few blocks to the town's private beach. As I turned onto Honeysuckle Road, my adrenaline started pumping. I had no idea what I'd find. I was a thousand percent sure I wouldn't like it though.

There wasn't a parking lot for the beach, so I pulled up parallel to it, my headlights catching a group of seven or eight kids huddled near the restrooms. As I stopped, I killed the lights, squinting through the darkness for a sign that one of them was my daughter.

Before I could decide my next move, my question was answered. Sam's snow-white knitted cap gave her away as she hurried across the moonlit sand toward me.

Relief that she was okay warred with anger and lingering fear for her safety. With the engine still running, I lowered the window, watching her every step.

When she was a few feet away, she whisper-demanded, "What are you doing here?"

"Get in the car, Samantha."

Her eyes narrowed as she stomped around the front to the passenger door.

"Thanks for ruining my life," she muttered as she got in.

"Follow the rules and I won't ruin your life." Clenching my jaw, I peered across the way at the group, but they'd drifted out of my line of sight, undoubtedly on purpose, and were likely on the other side of the restrooms.

Those kids weren't my problem.

Hell, that wasn't entirely true. "Do they have alcohol?" I asked Sam.

When she didn't answer, my tension crawled higher. I hadn't battled this one yet. I wasn't ready for it. This was my little girl. My formerly sweet daddy's girl who I could *not* let anything bad happen to.

"Samantha."

"I didn't drink anything," she said quietly, stopping me.

"You didn't?" I studied her profile across the front seat, assessing.

Her speech wasn't slurred or affected. I didn't smell alcohol. I would smell it, wouldn't I?

She didn't reply, but I suspected it was out of anger, not guilt.

Was I being naive?

I stared at her, searching for any signs I'd missed.

"What?" she bit out, whipping her head toward me.

What, indeed?

Where did I start? How did I handle this?

"I said I didn't drink anything." Every word was laced with indignation as she met my gaze.

Seconds ticked by as she glared at me.

"I believe you," I said.

As she looked away, she lowered her chin and crossed her arms. "Can we just go?"

I glanced toward the dark restrooms, which were closed for the winter. I didn't see any kids, but I was sure they were still there. "I should call the police."

"Oh, my God. Just kill me now."

"Don't say that."

"Don't be a nark. Haven't you destroyed my social life enough tonight?"

"Is Lacey there?"

My daughter went silent.

"She is," I guessed.

What the hell was the right move here? Should I call Lacey's mom? I didn't know the woman from Eve, but I had her number.

If our roles were reversed, I'd want a phone call. I'd want to know my daughter was on the beach drinking.

I pulled out my phone, located Lacey's mom's number, and hit Call. It went through on the Bluetooth, so the ringing sounded throughout the vehicle.

"*Dad, what are you doing?*" my daughter nearly shrieked. "Don't call the cops."

The call rang and rang. I put the SUV in gear and did a U-turn, driving toward home as I waited to leave a message, for whatever good that would do.

"Dad!"

The woman's voice mail message came on, short, sweet, not particularly confidence-inspiring.

"Hello," I said at the tone. "This is Chance Cordova, Sam's dad. We talked on New Year's Eve. I just wanted to let you know I found our daughters with a group on the beach. There's apparently alcohol involved. I'm taking Sam home, but the other kids are still there. I thought you should know."

"I doubt her mom will even care," Samantha said after I hit End.

"She doesn't care if her fourteen-year-old daughter gets drunk with a group that includes boys?"

"She trusts her daughter."

My brows shot up as I turned a corner. "Her trust is obviously misplaced."

Neither of us said anything for the rest of the short drive home. I was chewing over what my next move should be.

Once I'd parked in the garage and killed the engine, Sam shot out of the vehicle and stormed inside.

I sat there by the dim light of the garage door opener, biting the side of my mouth in frustration, wishing for a book with a list of effective parenting tips to fall into my lap.

When the light went off automatically and left me in the dark, I swore a blue streak under my breath and headed inside.

The kitchen hadn't been cleaned yet. Of course it hadn't. She'd had a beach party to sneak out to. But dirty pans were the least of my problems.

I strode down the stairs to her room.

Sam sat against her headboard, her phone cradled on her legs, attention fully on the screen. Her jaw was set in anger. So was mine.

I breathed in deeply and leaned against the wall, studying my daughter.

Puberty was a bitch. I knew friendships were tough to navigate, probably even more so for girls than boys. Add a new town and high school to the mix...

Damn, did I miss my little girl.

She'd never had an overload of friends back in Missouri, but the ones she'd had were good kids. She'd gotten excellent grades and liked learning. Where had we gone so wrong? Was this all because I'd moved her to a new town?

Tempering my tone, I asked, "What are you doing, Sam?"

Her gaze popped up to me for just an instant, as if the validity of the question got through to her. Sam was smart, so fucking smart, but lately she hadn't been acting like it, in the classroom or out. For that second, though, it was as if I reached the girl with the above-average brain.

Just as quickly, she shuttered her expression as if I were speaking a foreign language.

"I know how important friends are in high school, but Sam, these friends keep getting you in trouble. Is that what you want for yourself?"

She sat there, sullen and silent.

"Do you wait for me to leave so you can immediately break the rules and do exactly what I've told you a hundred times not to do? We don't have a long list of rules, Sam. I'm not being unreasonable by requiring you to get permission before leaving the house."

"You wouldn't let me go if I asked."

"Not to stand on the beach and drink," I said. "You're absolutely right. These girls... They don't seem like a very good choice in friends. You're smarter than this."

"Friends aren't about being smart," she snapped.

I stared at her, confused. "Do you look up to these people? You admire that they sneak out and get drunk? What is it that draws you to this group?"

"It doesn't matter," she said with venom in her voice. "I'm apparently not their friend anymore anyway." She indicated her phone and tossed it to the mattress. "They hate me thanks to you calling the cops."

"I didn't call the cops, Sam. You were right there with me."

"Well, someone did. They showed up right after we left, and now they think I'm a tattletale."

As much as I didn't approve of these kids, I hated that my daughter was hurting. I'd be ecstatic if she found someone new to be friends with.

"The police likely did a drive-by and saw them," I told her. "I didn't call anyone besides Lacey's mom."

"That doesn't really matter if they think I'm the nark."

A single tear rolled down her cheek, and I ached to pull her to me and hug away her sadness. Being a dad of a teen was a roller coaster ride that might well kill me before it was over.

Knowing she'd rebuke any attempt by me to comfort her, I stayed where I was, crossing my arms against the urge.

"I'm damn glad you were gone before the police arrived, but I'm sorry your friends are mad at you," I said.

She let out a hollow laugh. "They're not my friends anymore. So thanks for that."

More tears fell down her cheeks. I squeezed my eyes shut, exhausted, my heart breaking for my little girl. Fuck, I missed the days when I could make everything okay for her.

"Are these really the kinds of people you want to be friends with? People who blame you for something you didn't do?"

She didn't respond.

"Those aren't true friends, Sammy." Her childhood nickname popped out. I waited for her to scold me for using it, but she didn't. She just pulled her legs up and hugged them. "What happened to Kinsley?"

Kinsley had befriended my daughter when we first moved to Dragonfly Lake. She was a little bookish, shy, and had been kind to my daughter. I'd had no complaints about her, but I hadn't heard Sam mention her for ages.

"She's probably home studying," Sam said with a hint of derision in her tone.

"That's where you should've been. It's Thursday night. You're in high school. You're taking tough classes."

She shrugged.

Now wasn't the time for a lecture on studying, I decided.

I walked to the foot of her bed and sat down. "Hey," I said, gentling my voice.

Sam looked up at me.

"I'm proud of you for not drinking," I said. "That's not always an easy decision, particularly when everyone around you is doing it. You're a strong girl."

She pressed her lips together tightly as a new torrent of tears fell. "He... He kept pressuring me."

Anger snapped in me at whoever *he* was. "Pressuring you to do what?" The ideas going through my head weren't tolerable. "Sam," I said when she didn't answer, "what was he pressuring you to do?"

"To drink," she said.

"Is that all?"

She hesitated before saying, "That's all."

"Did he pressure you to do anything else?"

So help me, God, if he had...

Sam shook her head slowly, sadly. "No." She inhaled shakily, then said, "He said if I'd drink, maybe I'd lighten up."

This was what people meant when they talked about wanting to kill any teenage boy who came near their daughter. I'd like to break this fucker's neck.

Would it be wrong for a grown man to beat the hell out of a teenage punk?

I tried to calm down. Thank fuck I'd driven up when I had. Who knew what that little shit had planned for my daughter.

When I looked at her again, tears were streaming down her cheeks as she cried silently.

To hell with being careful around her. I moved closer and pulled her in for a hug, holding my breath, waiting to see if she'd push me away.

Even though she didn't hug me back, she buried her face against my chest and let out the sobs. I never knew my heart could ache with pain and explode with love at the same time.

"Let it out, Sammy," I whispered into her hair. "I got you."

In one night, my daughter had been pressured to drink by a boy, lost her group of friends, and been embarrassed by her dad picking her up. That was a rough time for a fourteen-year-old.

I hated all of it for her, but I wouldn't apologize for my part in it. And for the first time in months, she was letting me comfort her. That was progress. Maybe we could build on that going forward. With a teenager, baby steps were huge.

Chapter Nine

Rowan

The pregnancy test was wrong.

It had to be.

I sat down hard on the closed toilet in Chloe's bathroom, my mouth gaping.

There was a second line on the little wand, and there was nothing faint about it.

I couldn't process it.

A light knock sounded on the door.

"Rowan?" Presley said in a gentle voice. "You okay, hon?"

I took a breath to respond but realized I didn't have an answer.

"Ro?"

I stood, stepped to the door, opened it.

Presley looked me in the eyes, assessing. "I can't tell if that's a yes or a no."

Chloe approached from Sutton's bedroom, where she'd been putting her daughter to bed. "You don't look okay."

"I'm..." I shook my head. "I don't know what I am. How often do these things screw up?"

I picked up the test and held it out for them to see.

Presley gasped, and Chloe let out a controlled squeal. Then they continued to stare at me, as if waiting for me to confirm either reaction.

"It can't be right," I told them. "My doctor said... I made peace..." I stopped trying to get a coherent thought out and merely shook my head.

"I'm pretty sure false positives are really rare," Presley said.

"Less than one percent of the time," Chloe confirmed. "I've looked it up. You could take the second test."

"I don't think I can pee again," I said.

"Take it with you if you want," Chloe said. "Just for peace of mind."

"I will. Thanks."

"I think you're pregnant, hon," Presley said, watching me closely as she clasped my hand.

A mix of dread and hope trickled through me.

Chloe pulled out her phone, typed something in, and started reading causes of false positives. After each one, she looked at me. After each one, I shook my head. I wasn't on medications. I didn't have cysts as far as I knew. I hadn't been pregnant recently.

I looked down at the test again. There still an unmistakable second line staring back at me.

I squeezed my eyes shut, grasping the countertop when a wave of dizziness swept through me.

Presley's grip tightened. "Are you okay?"

I swallowed and nodded. "I think so. Can we sit down?"

"Yes. Good idea." Chloe led us out of the small bathroom.

Presley wound her arm through mine as we walked to the sofa.

"People say *I'm* hard to read," Chloe said as she sat on an armchair facing us.

"You are," Presley confirmed. "But Rowan's got you beat. Should we be offering a shoulder or tracking down some sparkling juice to celebrate?"

I folded my hands in front of my mouth, still trying to get the test results to sink in. "I'm afraid to hope, and this is probably the worst possible time in my life, but I've wanted babies for as long as I can remember."

"Oh, my God," Presley said, putting an arm around me from the side and leaning her head against my shoulder. "Congratulations, Rowan. I'm sorry the timing sucks, but I think you're getting your wish."

I met Chloe's gaze, most likely with a look of disbelief on my face. She was smiling and nodded, then came over to my other side.

"I think she's right. You have a little bean in there," she said.

"Wow," I said, because I couldn't figure out what else to say. It wasn't real yet. Not even close.

"I mean, you definitely need a doctor to confirm," Chloe said. "Take whatever time off you need for an appointment."

"Am I your first employee to take a pregnancy test in your home?" I asked her, grinning.

"We're friends first," she said, "thanks to this one." Chloe pointed at Presley.

I felt that too. Chloe treated me as more of an equal at work than an underling, even though I was only an assistant.

"My doctor's in Nashville," I said. "Unless... Is there an ob-gyn here?"

Chloe shook her head. "Just Dr. Julian. He's a wonderful family physician, but with your history..."

I nodded. "I need to see my regular doctor."

I imagined Dr. Shah's face as she confirmed the pregnancy. She was so compassionate and personable. I knew she'd understand the emotional complexity I was feeling.

I folded my hands in front of my mouth again and noticed, as my arms pressed into my chest, my breasts were tender.

"My boobs hurt," I said.

Both women's brows shot up, and smiles lit their faces again.

"Sure sign," Chloe said.

They leaned in for a group hug as I started to believe the test was correct.

"I can't even comprehend the odds," I said. "Not only did my doctor tell me it was highly unlikely to happen, but I had sex literally one time in the past two years. One time. Oh, and let me just add that we used a condom."

"Seems like not a very good one," Presley said.

"One time is all it takes," Chloe said.

"This baby is meant to be," Presley declared with conviction.

"If you wake up Sutton," Chloe said to her in a hushed voice, "you have to get her back to sleep."

"Kill joy." Presley leaned forward to stick her tongue out at Chloe. "I hesitate to bring this up, but what about the father, Rowan? Do you have a way to contact him?"

Shit on a shingle. I hadn't even thought about Chance yet. I was reeling too hard with the unlikeliness...and then the irony...

"I...do," I said.

"You got your one-night stand's number?" Presley asked.

"Something like that." I stood, suddenly feeling like I was going to come out of my skin. I paced from one side of the living room to the other. "I guess I'll have to tell him eventually."

"After the doctor confirms," Chloe said. "He deserves to know."

"And help pay," Presley added.

I shut down on thoughts of Chance for now. It was too much.

"I need to get health insurance," I said with a start.

"You don't have insurance?" Presley asked.

"I had to drop it after I quit teaching." My own health-care had inadvertently taken a back seat once I started caring for my grandmother. Thankfully I hadn't had any emergencies. I'd never intended to go so long without it, but I'd been in over my head with Gram's care from day one, and then money became a problem.

"Ours through work doesn't start until you've been there six months," Chloe said regretfully, "but you can get an individual policy."

"Yeah. I need to make that a priority." I knew it wouldn't be cheap. Nor would a place to live. Or all the baby gear. I wasn't sure my previous teaching salary would've covered it all, and I was making less now.

A wave of nausea came over me again, this time from overwhelm instead of food.

"I need to go," I said, then realized it was abrupt. "You guys have been a godsend. Thank you. For the dinner date and the tests and the support. I need to let this sink in."

"Of course," Chloe said. "We'll be here."

"Whatever you need." Presley leaned her head into me and side-hugged me again. "If you want someone to go with you to the doctor or need someone to buy more tests or want help researching insurance...anything...call me."

My eyes teared up with gratitude. "Thank you. I don't know what I need other than time to process."

"Understandable," Chloe said.

"If you start freaking out in the middle of the night, you can call me then too," Presley said as we all stood.

"I will. But I hope I'm asleep by then."

The three of us hugged again, and I held on tight to them, so thankful I'd reconnected with Presley at the exact right time.

"You two are the best," I said, meaning it. "I'm sorry to run off. I just...need to be alone."

"We get it," Chloe said.

I slid my coat on. "I'm going to call my doctor's office in the morning to see how soon I can get in."

"Let us know," Presley said. She threw her arms around me again. "You're gonna make an awesome mom."

My throat closed up with emotions, so I just nodded and waved at them both as I stepped outside.

On my way to my car, I sucked in deep breaths of ice-cold air, trying to level out the queasiness. I couldn't let my brain land on any of the thousand thoughts spinning through it.

Almost there, almost there, almost there. The words beat through my head with every step, my breaths in time with the rhythm as well.

By the time I got into my car, my eyes were a watery mess, my stomach was a bubbling volcano, and I raced to get the keys in the ignition.

Single Chance

Chloe and Holden's cute little house was only a mile from the inn, but halfway there I had to pull over. I scanned the street, grateful it was deserted, opened my car door, leaned out, and threw up everything in my stomach.

Chapter Ten

Chance

I jogged up the back stairs at the brewery a little after five p.m. Friday, still digesting the implications of my meeting with Holden and Chloe.

As I rounded the corner on the second floor, I could tell the light was still on in Rowan's office. Like always, anticipation pumped through me, and I had to shut down my involuntary eagerness to see her.

Over the past three weeks, we'd established a professional friendliness between us, an almost comfortable rapport. Almost. It'd be more comfortable if I could keep my mind from going where it shouldn't. From remembering flashes of New Year's Eve. From fantasizing about another hookup.

With Holden and Chloe hurrying off to pick up their daughter for some family event in the city tonight and Mateo on the road, the only other person in the building was Kemp, who was in the brewhouse. Rowan and I practically had the place to ourselves.

Which meant nothing at all.

I prepared to smile, wish her a happy weekend, and walk past her open door toward my own office. Except when I peered in, I stopped in my tracks. She had her head down on her desk, face buried in her arms.

"Rowan?" I said from the doorway.

She raised her head and blinked sleepily. "Hi."

I stepped inside. "Are you okay?"

She inhaled as if assessing, then nodded. "I didn't sleep much last night. I put my head down to rest my eyes for five minutes."

"It's almost five thirty. Weekend time."

"I told Chloe I'd stay late to prep for tomorrow's tour since she gave me the morning off."

"She said you had a last-minute appointment in Nashville this morning." I couldn't help prying. I'd noticed Rowan's absence and been relieved when I heard her voice in the hallway early this afternoon.

She eyed me tiredly. Assessing me. For what, I couldn't guess.

"Is everything okay, Rowan?"

She didn't respond, seemingly deliberating with herself. I took another step toward her desk, confused, my concern growing.

"Yeah." She flashed a tired smile. "I'm good. What are you doing working late?"

"Just got done with a meeting. I'd ask you if you read Chloe's email yet, but I'm thinking you haven't checked lately." I grinned to make it clear I wasn't judging her for resting. I couldn't help but notice the shadows beneath her eyes.

"Email about what?"

I sat in the chair facing her desk. "She has too much on

her plate, and she knows it. Holden convinced her to hand off everything marketing related to you."

Her eyes locked on mine as the ramifications sank in.

"Marketing," she repeated. "You're the marketing director."

"Chloe's been in on everything as we've developed the brand. But that's pretty much established now. The next thing will be rolling out the event venue campaign."

"So I'll be working with you," she concluded, not smiling.

"I've been told I'm decent to work with."

"You all realize I know nothing about marketing, right?"

"You'll do fine. As long as you can work directly with me?"

For the first time, I wondered if she was more uncomfortable than I'd realized because of our history. She'd seemed to handle working for the same company okay, as if our night together had been almost nothing. That sucked for me, but it was better than the opposite extreme. I did not need a clinger.

When she didn't reply, just continued sizing me up, my concern grew.

"Rowan? What's going through your head?"

She averted her eyes and bit her lower lip, then straightened as if making a decision. "Could you close the door?"

I frowned, unease exploding in my gut. Instead of mentioning there was no one left in this part of the building, I stood and did as she asked. Retaking my seat, I said, "What's going on?"

Rowan leaned her elbows on her desk and ran her hands over her face. As she lowered them, she nailed me with intense but tired brown eyes.

"There's no way to ease into this," she said, sitting up

straighter. "And this isn't the right place for this discussion, but I'm not sure there is a right place. I'm pregnant, Chance."

That explained why she was so tired, and maybe why she'd had a last-minute appointm—

Wait.

Hold the fucking phone.

Was she suggesting...

"How pregnant?" I stupidly asked.

Rowan glanced at her desk calendar. "Twenty-four days."

The chair flew backward as I stood abruptly, unable to remain calm as her implication became clear. "It's... I'm... From New Year's?"

She nodded. "From New Year's."

I paced the narrow width of the room. "That's not possible. We used protection."

She let out a laugh that had an edge of hysteria to it. "You don't even know the half of it."

I pivoted to her, confused. "What do you mean?"

Rowan inhaled deeply, glancing at the ceiling before meeting my gaze. "I have endometriosis. My ob-gyn told me when I was twenty-six years old it would be highly unlikely I'd have children, at least not without a procedure, which I haven't had."

I tried to puzzle through that. I'd heard of the condition but didn't know a lot about it. My feet carried me back to the chair in front of her, and I sat down hard. "So you aren't likely to conceive. We used birth control. And still—"

"I'm pregnant. My doctor confirmed it this morning. I was able to get in on someone else's cancelation."

"Jesus." I absently rubbed my jaw as I tried to get the storm in my head under control. "For sure New Year's?"

She tilted her head and shot me a fake, sugary-sweet grin. "Only time I've been with someone for more than two years."

"Sorry," I said, realizing that was an insensitive question. "I'm just having a hard time wrapping my head around this."

"You and me both."

"I'm guessing, since you told me, you're planning to keep the baby?"

"Yes," she said with no hesitation. "The timing is terrible, but this could be my only chance to be a mom."

I nodded and tried to imagine having a baby again. *A baby.* For fuck's sake, I was in way over my head with the teenager I had.

She picked up a pen and tapped the end on the desk. "If you don't want to be in the baby's life—"

"I didn't say that."

"I know. I'm just acknowledging how awkward this is."

"I..." I shook my head, leaned forward, elbows on knees. Let out a hollow laugh. "This'll take a bit to sink in."

"Tell me about it."

I glanced up at her again, struck anew by those shadows under her eyes. I pulled my thoughts away from myself for a minute as I studied her more closely. "This is why you didn't sleep much last night."

"Yep." Her lips fluttered upward briefly in a smile attempt that didn't quite work.

In that moment, she looked so young, so vulnerable. I was overcome by the urge to go to her, pull her into my arms, and tell her everything would be okay. That could be stretching the truth though, because who knew how any of it would turn out?

"Does anyone else know?" I asked.

"Chloe and Presley were with me when I tested."

My eyes went wide. Our boss hadn't even hinted that something was off.

"They don't know it's you," she added in a rush. "That's a whole different mess."

Mess, indeed.

"We'll get to that eventually, huh? How are you holding up?" I asked.

"Life is weird." She shrugged. "I have a lot to figure out. Everything from health insurance to a place to live to my career. My due date is September twenty-third. Just in time for back to school."

"Shit," I said.

"In spite of all that"—she smiled, and it seemed only a little forced—"this baby's a miracle I was told I might never have."

I might not know her well, but in that instant I had zero doubts she'd be one hell of a mom.

An image of her holding a newborn, gazing at him or her with love, popped into my head, and damn if that didn't shake me on multiple levels.

A baby. A child. Rowan was getting her chance to be a mother. And fuck me running, I was going to be a father again.

My phone vibrated in my pocket. I pulled it out, relieved for the distraction. It was from my daughter.

Sam: Can we have Humble's tonight?

I stared at the words, unable to remember the last time Sam willingly reached out to me. And about dinner, no less.

"Is everything okay?" Rowan asked. "I mean, excepting our situation, of course. With the message?"

I managed a half smile. "Excepting our situation. It's my daughter, Sam. She wants me to bring pizza home with me. She doesn't normally even want to talk to me."

"You should get home to her."

Inviting Rowan to join us crossed my mind, but I dismissed it. Last night had ended with my daughter opening up to me in a small but significant way. Bringing a stranger home for dinner was a surefire way to ruin that progress.

Fuck. I'd eventually have to come clean to Sam about Rowan. That I'd gotten her pregnant. There was no way that would go over well.

One night of fun, and we'd fucked ourselves well and good and created one hell of a tough situation. I couldn't fix it tonight. I couldn't even comprehend all the pieces of it tonight.

Pizza first. I could handle pizza.

I replied to Sam.

> Chance: Pepperoni and mushrooms?

> Sam: Yes.

> Chance: I'll order one and pick it up on my way home. See you soon.

"You said your daughter's fourteen?" Rowan asked.

"Right."

She cringed. "A baby could make her feel threatened."

Threatened, pissed, insecure, betrayed... Telling my daughter would be one of the hardest things I'd had to do in my life.

"Yeah," was all I said. "I need some time to think. Then you and I need to have some conversations."

Rowan nodded. "Yes."

I didn't know how anything was going to work out, but the one thing I was damn sure of as the facts began to sink in was that, if there was a kid with my genes and my blood, I would do my best by him or her. "I want to be in this baby's life."

Chapter Eleven

Rowan

By early Saturday afternoon, I still couldn't get the intense look on Chance's face out of my mind. The one when he'd said, with conviction, that he wanted to be in the baby's life.

I'd lain awake for hours again last night, my brain chugging overtime, sorting through all the decisions to be made. Feeling alone. Overwhelmed. And yes, remembering Chance's expression. Trying to push it aside. Trying not to be affected by it. It wasn't just about how damn appealing he was to me on a physical basis or how handsome. A man who felt fiercely responsible for a baby he'd helped conceive? *That* was sexy.

Would his sense of responsibility infringe on my ability to parent? That remained to be seen. We hadn't begun to discuss how to make it work. I didn't feel threatened by his interest. To me, that was a sign of a caring, accountable man.

We'd created this baby together, and I was hopeful that

we could work out an agreement with the baby's best interests at heart. My gut told me Chance was a reasonable man. I'd give him the benefit of the doubt until he gave me reason to think otherwise.

I'd come to Dragonfly Lake to focus on my needs, to reconnect with myself, so today I was trying to do exactly that while distracting myself from my thoughts. I'd come downtown to explore the shops.

I focused on my glorious surroundings: racks of gorgeous handmade paper, shelves teeming with beautiful notebooks, an entire wall of colorful pens... The Lily Pad stationery store was just as dangerous as I'd imagined all those weeks I'd refused to let myself stop in.

I might not have much money for a treat, but my office-supply-loving heart got a thrill just browsing this unique store. And yes, I was allowing myself to spend a little. While some girls' retail therapy was a splurge on a new pair of shoes, my happy place was right here in this charming shop.

I planned to keep a pregnancy journal, and I'd need notebooks to organize the gargantuan changes in my life. And pens... You could never have too many pens. I was overdue to restock. When you spent your days devising distractions to keep a dementia patient calm and your nights half-listening for said patient to wander the house, pens and notebooks became irrelevant and forgotten.

I took my selections to the checkout counter and handed them over to the thirty-something strawberry blonde with porcelain skin. If I wasn't mistaken, she also worked at the inn. I'd seen her at the front desk some evenings when I came in from work, said hello a few times.

"These pens are the best," she said as she rang up each of them.

"I hope so. The brand is new to me."

"You're Rowan, right?"

"That's right," I said.

"I'm friends with Chloe. My name is Magnolia."

"Nice to meet you. You work at the Honeysuckle Inn too?"

"That's right."

"Do you ever sleep?" I asked.

She laughed. "Not very well. I heard you might be looking for a place to live?"

"Yes," I said. "Do you know of something?"

"Possibly someone looking for a roommate."

"Oh." I tried to keep my disappointment out of my voice, but a roommate wouldn't work. Not unless they were open to sharing space with a newborn.

"I heard Harper Ellison is moving in with her fiancé, so her roomie, Dakota, might be looking for someone. They have an apartment here on the square, above Earthly Charm."

"Great location," I said noncommittally. It sounded perfect...except for the roommate. I didn't know Dakota, but even if she was a baby lover with the patience of a saint, I'd never feel comfortable bringing a baby home with a roommate.

"Would you like me to pass her your contact info?"

"Not yet," I hedged. *Think fast.* "I'm hoping for no roommates. I'm up in the middle of the night a lot and would hate to bother someone."

Magnolia laughed again. "Too bad I don't have room for you in my apartment. We could be insomniacs together."

"Right," I said with a smile. "Do you live nearby?"

"Right upstairs." She gestured above us. "But it's tiny.

Dotty, who owns this shop, uses part of the upstairs for storage."

"Well, at least you don't have a long commute."

"Those are hard to find in Dragonfly Lake."

Once she'd checked me out, I told her I'd let her know if I changed my mind about roommates and Dakota. "Thanks for telling me about her."

"Of course. Enjoy your goodies."

There were definitely good parts of living in a small town, I thought as I exited the Lily Pad. The people were friendly, and even strangers acted more like neighbors. I'd been fairly isolated for two years, so I treasured the connections.

There was also a downside of small-town living. My pregnancy wouldn't stay secret or anonymous for long. If Chance meant what he'd said, our hookup would become common knowledge. I'd either need to prepare myself for that or get the hell out of town. I was leaning hard toward preparing for that, because as uncomfortable as it might be at first, I was falling for this place.

I took a right on the sidewalk and passed Lake Girl Boutique next. The clothes in the window were cute, but I wasn't in clothes shopping mode.

I crossed to the next block, inhaling the sweet aromas coming from Sugar and fighting off temptation. I made it past the door like a champion and kept walking to the next shop—and froze in my tracks as I caught sight of...a llama? I thought it was a llama, but my llama identification skills were untried.

Whatever it was, it was coming straight toward me on the sidewalk, looking like it was on a mission. The door to the next store was within reach, so I yanked it open and hurried inside as the furry white beast got closer.

"Oh, there goes Esmerelda," a voice said from somewhere inside the store.

I looked out the front window as the llama pranced past. With my mouth hanging open, I whipped my head around to find the woman who'd spoken.

"Good afternoon," the older woman with blond-highlighted hair said as she walked toward me. "I see you nearly met our local llama on the run."

"You know the llama?" I asked, glancing out the window again but seeing no trace of the animal now.

"Everyone knows Esmerelda. She belongs to Dr. Holloway, the veterinarian." She laughed and shook her head. "I guarantee you she's camped out in front of the bakery by now, waiting for that door to open. It's the rainbow-sprinkled sugar cookies she's after."

"That's relatable," I said, still wrapping my head around coming face-to-face with a llama in a small town.

"Welcome to Fat Cat Yarn. I'm Loretta."

"Rowan," I said, finally taking in the racks and racks of yarn in every color. "Wow."

The outer walls were floor-to-ceiling cubbies of yarn forming a rainbow of hues from one end to the other. The interior had more racks that were shoulder-high, filled by still more colors and types of yarn.

As I skimmed my gaze over the expanse of variegated skeins on the nearest rack, something brushed against my pants leg, startling me.

"Oh!" I pressed my hand to my heart when I spotted the chunky gray cat who'd sideswiped me on its way past. "Look at you."

"That's Purl. She doesn't mean to be rude, but you caught her between her lunch and her afternoon nap in the window display."

"Naps are important," I said, watching the chubby cat waddle to the window and jump up on a cat perch.

"To Purl, naps are everything. Well, and tuna. Are you a knitter, my dear? Crochet?"

"Well..." I glanced around again, the colorful yarn awakening my creativity much in the same way the paper store had. "Calling me a knitter would be an exaggeration." I stepped down the aisle in her direction, to a section of muted, variegated pastel-toned skeins that screamed baby blankets. "My grandmother taught me, but I never fully mastered it." I smiled, running my fingers over the soft skeins, my chest aching as I remembered Gram's infinite patience as she taught me, then sat next to me as I practiced, answering my questions or fixing my mistakes when I made them—and I made a lot of them.

"Oh, how sweet she was able to share that with you. Her legacy was teaching you what she loved?"

"She did love to knit. She had Alzheimer's, and that's something it took from her in her last few years. She died in December."

"That's heartbreaking," Loretta said.

I nodded, drawn to a particular yarn with lavender, mint, and cream variations. "She had a closet full of yarn," I said. "During one of her clearer days, she asked me to donate it all to a local knitting club, so I did. This is so pretty."

"That makes the softest blankets."

I picked up a skein, my mind churning. My baby would need a blanket. If Gram were alive and well, she'd knit a special one.

Grief gathered in my throat, and my eyes went teary. I kept my gaze averted, running my fingers over the yarn that was indeed remarkably soft. "I'd like to make a baby blanket, but I'm not sure I could pull it off." I laughed quietly, mostly to divert myself from crying. Then I added, "I know someone who's pregnant."

"I'd be happy to help you. We have knitting groups where we help anyone who needs it."

I considered the idea. "I need so much help I'd be annoying."

"Never," Loretta said. "We were all beginners at some point. Most of us had someone to help us. For me it was my mother."

"Do any groups meet on weekends or in the evening?"

She tilted her head sympathetically. "I'm afraid not. Our demographics are retirees and a couple young mothers."

I nodded, disappointed, because the more I thought about it, the more I wanted to knit my baby a blanket. In honor of my grandmother. It would be connecting the past with the future.

"I'll tell you what though," Loretta said. "If you'd like to learn, I'll meet you here any time you want—except Thursday evenings. Thursdays are when the Dragonfly Diamonds meet, and I can't miss that. I'll help you with a blanket."

"Dragonfly Diamonds?"

She chuckled. "A bunch of us ladies like to get together to play a little poker."

"Good for you," I said, thinking I'd never met anyone like Loretta. Gram would've liked her too.

I made eye contact, hoping she wouldn't notice the teary remnants. "You'd really sacrifice your time to help me?"

"It wouldn't be a sacrifice." Her smile was kind, forming

deep crinkles at the corners of her eyes. "It would give me such joy."

I studied her face, looking for any hint she didn't mean it, but all I saw was kindness.

"Knitting is good for the soul, Rowan," she continued. "It's been shown to lower stress levels and decrease anxiety. I find it therapeutic. It's soothing, something you can do for the rest of your life. It'd be my pleasure to refresh your grandmother's gift to you."

"I can tell you're passionate about it."

"Passionate." She laughed. "Honey, I sank everything I had into opening up this little shop just so I could share it with others, create a gathering place, a community of creative souls who like to keep their hands busy."

I read the yarn label, not really remembering anything Gram had taught me to look for. "You said this would work for a blanket?"

"That's a four weight. It'll be perfect."

I'd barely had time to imagine a tiny baby in a crib. *My* tiny baby in a crib in *my* home, wherever that ended up being. But that's what I wanted. My baby in my home with a beautiful blanket stitched with love. I nodded. "If you're serious, I'll take you up on it."

Loretta took the skein from me to read it, did some figuring in her head, then said, "You'll need about four skeins for a baby blanket. You can pick a time whenever you're ready, and we'll get you started."

She took me to the next room, where there was a long table with comfortable-looking chairs around it and containers of scissors and knitting needles scattered on top. The walls were covered with more yarn, needles, scissors, books, and other supplies I couldn't name.

Once I had the supplies she recommended, I paid at the counter in the front room.

"You just let me know when you settle on a time," she said.

"Thank you," I said. "I can't wait to get started."

"We'll have fun."

We said goodbye, and I walked back outside, darting a glance toward the bakery, scanning for the llama. That's when I noticed traffic was stopped, a small crowd had gathered on the other side of the street, and a guy was guiding the llama away from the bakery.

This town was something else. I was beginning to think it was something special. Maybe exactly what I needed.

Just today I'd met a pen-loving girl who'd tried to help with my search for a place to live and a kind woman who was willing to help me honor my sweet Gram.

If Loretta could work a miracle, maybe I'd gained a new hobby. A soothing, stress-reducing one. God knows I needed it to keep me from freaking out about being pregnant and worrying about having a baby with a man I barely knew.

Chapter Twelve

Chance

Our single dad group wasn't the same as it used to be. Still good, still some of the best friends I had. But our Saturday nights had definitely changed.

Given that three of the six of us had done away with the "single" designation, it wasn't surprising. Our weekly Saturdays had recently shifted to biweekly out of necessity. Whereas the big challenge used to be finding babysitters for everyone's kids, now Knox, Max, and Ben had wives or fiancées to stay with their kids, but that meant their houses wouldn't work as a gathering spot most weekends. It also meant they often had to work around family plans.

I used to host frequently because our basement had been set up for it with a pool table, dartboard, and big screen, but recently I'd agreed to let Sam take over the basement as her space, hoping if I showed her a little trust and gave her some independence, she'd use it wisely. Her bedroom was now one end of the L-shaped lower level, giving her one hell of a teenage domain. Tonight she had plans to binge as many seasons of *Gilmore Girls* as she could on the big screen.

My daughter's so-called friends had indeed written her off after their Thursday night drinking session on the beach had gotten busted. They didn't care that she hadn't ratted them out. Even my call to Lacey's mother hadn't been what got them in trouble. The cops had discovered them without any help. The result was that Lacey and the mean girls she hung out with no longer wanted anything to do with Sam.

I hated that Sam was hurting, but I believed those girls —and the boys they snuck out to drink with—weren't the right people for her. She'd spent Friday night at home in the basement away from me—but still home, where I knew she was safe—not drinking and not dealing with some little asswipe pressuring her to do... I couldn't let myself think too hard about what he might've had in mind for her.

The dads and I had agreed to meet at Elliott's, a dive bar off the beaten track with multiple TVs, damn good wings, and none of the twenty-something meat-market crowd the Barn Bar and the Fly tended to attract.

Some nights we planned our evening around a particular sports event. Tonight it'd been the Predators game, which had ended in a victory.

Our gatherings didn't usually last too late, as we all had kids to get home to and babysitters to relieve. Once tonight's game ended, we'd finished our drinks, talked hockey for a few minutes, and now here we were, headed out the door of Elliott's before ten thirty p.m.

"Look at you fuckers, all eager to get home to your ladies," West said as the five of us—Luke was home with a sick kid—walked out the door.

"Accurate," Max said. "That was a hell of a game. The

company was good as always. But it's cold as a son of a bitch out here, and I can't wait to get home to my warm bed."

"And the fiancée waiting for you in it," Knox said.

"That's the hope." Max laughed.

"When's Harper moving in officially?" Ben asked.

"Not soon enough," Max said as we stood in a clump outside the door of the bar. "She doesn't want to leave Dakota hanging."

"I bet she'll be able to find someone to sublease pretty fast," Ben said. "Somebody needs to build a new apartment complex in this town. Housing's starting to be a problem."

"That housing problem got you a wife," West pointed out, and we all laughed.

Ben had taken in his friend Emerson and her kids while she hunted for a place to live. Before she could find something in her budget, they'd fallen in love and gotten married at the courthouse.

"We might be heading home earlier than I used to start back when I was in college, but I'm glad we made it work tonight," Knox said.

"Good times as always," West said.

We all said our goodbyes. Then Knox, Max, and Ben, who'd parked on the street, walked in one direction while West and I went toward the small lot behind.

"You okay tonight?" West asked as we made our way between the buildings.

"Why wouldn't I be?" I pulled my stocking cap down farther as we emerged to the back side and got smacked by a cold gust of wind.

"You're quiet. Seemed lost in thought more than once during the game."

"I'm fine," I lied. I kept hoping if I told myself that, it'd start being true. So far, no dice.

"You pissed about those little shits that hurt Sam?"

I'd told the guys about Thursday and how her friends had dropped her.

"I wouldn't mind throwing the one little punk into the middle of the lake with a concrete block tied around his neck," I admitted.

"My girls aren't allowed out of the house till they're twenty."

I laughed. "Good luck with that."

"Sam's still home?" he asked.

Pulling out my phone, I opened the app to locate her. She hadn't moved. I held it up to West.

"So it's not her that's got you upset," he said.

"I'm not upset," I snapped.

West looked over at me with his brows halfway up his forehead.

"Hell," I said, knowing full well I was being a dick. "Do you need to get home to the girls?"

He checked the time. "I told the babysitter I'd be there by eleven. You want to come over for a beer?"

As much as I hated to admit it, I needed to bounce some thoughts off someone before my head blew up. "Sure."

"I'll meet you there." West got in his truck.

I went to my SUV and followed him to his place. I wouldn't stay long. I wanted to get home to check in with Sam. Maybe she'd let me watch an episode or two with her. I couldn't care less about the Gilmores, but I hated that my daughter might be lonely or sad.

West lived in a tiny two-bedroom house with his three little girls—seven-year-old twins, Scarlett and Sienna, and four-year-old Nova. I couldn't imagine how cramped they'd been when his ex was still his live-in girlfriend. But they made do. His daughters were growing up in a house filled with love, regardless of the size of it.

Once he'd let me in, he got the report from Allison, a high-schooler who watched his kids frequently, settled up with her, then peeked in the girls' room. I heard the bedroom door squeak as he closed it.

"Sleeping like angels," he said quietly as he reentered the galley-style kitchen. He opened the refrigerator and took out two Rusty Anchor bottles.

"Thanks," I said. "Your sitter seems like a good one."

"She's a gem. I'd like to hire her for the summer full-time. Their daycare is breaking the bank."

"It was a lot of money for just one kid back when Sam went. I don't know how you manage three."

He swept out his arm. "Livin' in a shoebox is how." His eyes sparkled as he said it, telling me without words it wasn't a hardship and he'd do whatever he needed to for those little girls.

"You ready to spill whatever's up your ass?" he asked, then took a drink.

I hoisted myself up to the counter and grabbed my beer like a lifeline. "I've got a situation."

"What the hell does that mean?" He followed suit, sitting across from me, his burly body taking up the entire space between the sink and refrigerator.

"I don't need to tell you this is all confidential, right?"

He brushed me off like I was being stupid. "No shit."

I took a big swallow of Kayak Smack Ale, holding the bitter liquid on my tongue for a moment. Kemp and our people knew how to brew a damn good ale.

I returned my attention to West's impatient face. "New Year's Eve," I said simply.

Though West had taken off just before midnight that

night, he'd given me plenty of hell about my interest in Rowan, but he wasn't a gossip or a big mouth. As far as I knew, he'd not broadcast my business to anyone after I'd admitted to going to her room.

"The mystery girl," he said.

"Who ended up working at the brewery."

He narrowed his eyes at me. "You didn't tell me that. How the hell haven't I heard about this?"

"Nobody seems to have figured out she and I were together that night. By some stroke of luck, no one from work was at the inn's party." I shook my head. In this town it was a bigger surprise if a secret *didn't* get out.

"Holy shit balls, bro. You work with your one-night stand?" He started to lift his bottle to his mouth and stopped. "Or was it not just one night? You still fucking her?"

"I'm not fucking her."

His grin widened. "What are the odds of her working for your very small employer?"

Odds indeed.

"That's not the situation," I said, once again causing him to lower his beer bottle with his curious gaze locked on me.

His brows rose as he waited me out.

"She's pregnant."

"You. Are. Shitting. Me." He emphasized each word. "Why the hell didn't you wrap it before you tapped it, Chance?"

"I fucking wrapped it, asshole." Possibly with an out-of-date condom, I'd realized belatedly.

"Oh, fuck. What are you gonna do?"

I shook my head because I didn't have an answer yet.

"She's gonna keep it?" he asked.

"Yep." I refused to share Rowan's personal health issues with him.

He studied me for a good long while, then said, "You want me to get the whiskey out?"

I'd tried that last night after Sam had gone to bed. It had solved nothing. I shook my head.

"She was in a vulnerable spot even before this," I said. "Her grandmother died in December of Alzheimer's. Rowan was the woman's twenty-four-hour caretaker. I don't know details, but she's been through a shit storm. She's living at the inn, trying to find a place to rent. She doesn't have health insurance, doesn't have much money."

"What's she want from you?" West asked.

"Nothing so far." I didn't get the impression she was the type to ask for anything.

He narrowed his eyes. "How well do you know her?"

I laughed. "I know her as a coworker, and I know the sounds she makes when she comes apart. Not much in between." I fought not to let myself think about those sounds every damn night.

West looked thoughtful as he raised his bottle for another drink. I did the same.

"Do you think I should offer to marry her?" I asked after swallowing a gulp.

He slammed his bottle down on the counter next to him. "Fuck no, you shouldn't. Don't you dare."

I hadn't expected the fierceness of his reply, but West wasn't one to keep his opinion to himself.

"She doesn't have insurance or money," I said. "She could move in rent-free. I could make sure she's eating well and doing healthy stuff for the baby."

"She can get her own insurance policy without marrying your dumb ass."

"It'll be expensive."

"For fuck sure. But so would a divorce."

"Okay, so I don't need to marry her." That was a relief if I was honest.

"Sure as shit don't." West scoffed. "If you suggested marrying her, you'd come across as a chest-beating control freak who doesn't think she can make it on her own."

I considered that and realized he could be right. Control wasn't what drove me. I wanted to help her out. But I could see where that could be misinterpreted. "So what do I do then?"

"You've decided you're gonna be in the kid's life?"

I nodded. West did too.

"She can sign up for insurance," he said.

"I'll offer her our spare bedroom."

West scoffed. "How's that gonna play with Sam?"

I clenched my jaw tight because that was a prime concern. "I'm in a tight spot. Sam and I had a minor breakthrough the other night when she let me comfort her."

"And now you wanna move in your lady."

"Rowan is *not* my lady."

"Just your baby mama." West shook his head as if I was screwed, which I pretty much was.

"I won't tell Sam that right away. I'll give her some time to get used to Rowan."

"You think Rowan will go for this plan?"

"I don't think she has much of a choice. You know how tough it is to find a long-term rental here."

"I don't know your lady—"

"She's not my lady," I repeated.

"But nobody likes to feel cornered."

"I'm not cornering her. I'm offering her a solution to a problem."

He eyed me, nodding, looking pensive. "Say she says yes, moves in, somehow Sam comes around. Rowan gets big with your baby. You work together, live together, go to child-birth classes together. You really think you're not gonna fall for this girl?"

I was worried as fuck about falling for this girl, but I'd get through being roommates. It wouldn't be forever.

"Would you suggest I just leave her to live in some shitty apartment with black mold and leaky windows while she brews my child?" I shot back.

"Fuck. Course not. I don't think you have much of a choice but to offer."

"That's the conclusion I keep coming to."

"But don't fucking marry her."

I nodded, knowing he was right.

I wouldn't admit it out loud even at gunpoint, but there was a small, dumbass part of me that had gotten a thrill at the thought of Rowan being my wife. It made no sense at all. I wasn't in the market. I was dad to a teenage handful who needed all my attention and love. Serious relationships weren't an option.

If Rowan said yes to moving in, the next few months were going to be hairy as hell. I'd have to play the balancing act of a lifetime.

I guessed this was what I got for one night of fun.

Chapter Thirteen

Rowan

At work on Monday, I ended a marathon call with a health insurance person and resisted the urge to wilt onto my desk. Having Chance catch me midsnooze on Friday evening had been embarrassing enough. I'd only been resting for five minutes when he'd found me, but it didn't look good.

Chloe was turning out to be a goddess of a boss. When she'd found out this morning I hadn't been able to secure health insurance during weekend hours, she'd ordered me to take the time to call a broker today, so I had. But I didn't want to take advantage of her boundless empathy and understanding.

As I eyed the monthly premium amount I'd jotted on a sticky note, I tapped my pen on the desk in a rapid, nervous rhythm.

Health insurance was a whopper of an expense on a budget like mine, but it wasn't one I could delay. I'd signed up for a plan on the spot. If that financial commitment meant sleeping in my car, then I'd be sleeping in my car.

I'd spent yesterday searching for a place to live, as my one-month stay at the inn, which Ava had given me yet another break on, was up in a few days. I could spring for another week there, or a month if I had to, but it'd mean dipping into the rapidly dwindling fund from Gram's belongings. It had me considering every possible option.

I'd made an appointment tomorrow to see a garage apartment over lunch. It was a studio, not ideal once the baby came, but what made me even more reluctant was that the place looked run-down in the photos, with a water stain on the ceiling and windows that appeared ancient and leaky. I'd give it a chance though. My choices were limited.

Maybe the Dakota person who lived above Earthly Charm would consider letting me room with her until my baby was born. Probably not, and I didn't even know what the rent was to live with her. With that premium location? It was probably out of my reach, even with a roommate.

This evening's project would be fine-tuning my budget...if I could summon the energy. Between the pregnancy itself sapping my energy, the stress that came with finding out about it, and lying awake for hours each night trying to process my new reality, I was beyond exhausted. It took me back to the hardest times with Gram, when she had her worst, most agitated days that took every ounce of fortitude I had to get through them.

This isn't the same, I reminded myself. *This isn't caring for a confused, dying woman. This is setting up the future for a new life.*

That truth brought a smile to my face, but it didn't make me any less drained.

Maybe tonight I would sleep.

The body had to win out over the brain and fall into near-unconsciousness to reboot eventually, didn't it?

"Hey, marketing assistant." Chance appeared in my doorway, looking delectable in a navy blazer, a white button-down shirt, no tie, and jeans that fit his muscled thighs just right.

"Hi. Is that my official title now?"

His lips eased into a slow, dimpled smile that made my mouth go dry. "Nah. Not official. But selfishly speaking, I like the sound of it. What are you doing for lunch?"

"Lunch?" I asked stupidly. I glanced at my phone screen and saw it was eleven thirty. "I didn't realize it was this late. I brought a sandwich."

"PB and J?"

Our gazes met for a moment as if he was in on one of my secrets. My sandwich of choice was the least sensitive of my secrets that he was in on actually.

"PB and J," I confirmed. "With a side of veggies and guac."

"Leave that for tomorrow. I'm treating you today. Marketing lunch."

I studied him, trying to ascertain if he was speaking as my boss—was he my boss now?—or as the father of my baby or as a friend. His brows rose in question as he waited for me to respond. I decided it didn't matter, as we had a lot of ground to cover, both professionally and personally.

"Marketing lunch," I repeated. "Sure. Right now?"

"Can you get away now?"

"I can. Is anyone else going?"

He shook his head, glanced both directions in the hall, leaned in, and said, "You and I have a lot to talk about." His private tone told me it wouldn't be all marketing.

"We do." I stood, picked up my purse and coat, and joined him in the hall.

"I told Holden and Chloe I'm going to get you up to speed on the venue project," he said as we descended the stairs to the first floor.

I took his cue and made small talk about the brewery's potential for events like weddings and parties until we were closed in his SUV against the biting January day. Once it was just us, I let out a quiet, uncertain breath.

"It's nerve-racking, isn't it?" he asked. "Hiding a whopper of a secret from everyone at work?"

"Yeah," I said, surprised to hear him voice my thoughts. "I thought maybe it was partly because I'm the new girl."

Chance chuckled. "Not because you're the new girl." He started the engine, adjusted the heat setting, then took out his phone. "First things first, can I get your number? We need a way to communicate outside of work. I didn't figure me showing up at the inn whenever I had a question would work."

"Probably not." His surprise visit on my first day of work had conjured vivid memories of New Year's Eve. Scene of the crime, so to speak.

I took his phone from him, entered my number, and handed it back.

He sent me a message so I'd have his number as well, then put the SUV into gear and drove us out of the parking lot.

"Where are we going?" I asked when he drove through the square and didn't turn in at the diner or the street to Humble's.

Chance glanced across the front seat at me. "I wanted to talk privately, so if you don't mind, I can whip up something for us at my house."

"You're going to cook?"

"Chicken and pasta with a garlic cream sauce. Does that sound okay?"

My day had taken a turn I hadn't expected at all, but then so had my life. We did need privacy. "It sounds okay," I confirmed, curious about his cooking skills even as my stomach gurgled with a hint of nausea at the mention of heavy food.

"Just food and discussion. I know it's sketchy to take you to my home, but this town has big ears, and so does my daughter."

"She's at school?"

"She better be."

That was an interesting response. My curiosity about her grew. I could get along well with most teenagers in my classroom. It remained to be seen how I'd do with the daughter of my baby's father. We wouldn't be starting off with a blank slate...*if* I even got to meet her.

Chance pulled into the driveway of a two-story home in a family neighborhood. He parked in the attached garage and led me into the house. I followed him through a laundry room into the kitchen, which was big by my standards and reasonably clean. There was a short dining bar between it and a dining nook.

"Welcome to my humble home," he said as he took off his coat and laid it over the back of one of the barstools.

When he held out a hand for my coat, I slid it off and gave it to him.

"Your home is nice," I said.

"I can show you around after we eat if we have time."

"You moved here after your wife died?" I asked, my curiosity overriding my hesitancy to bring up a sad subject.

"Several years after."

I watched his face as I sat on one of the stools, trying to read him, wondering whether this was a taboo subject. He gave away nothing. "Was she sick?" I asked.

He turned his back to me and opened the refrigerator, took out chicken and a few ingredients, and set them on the counter. Without making eye contact, he answered, "She was addicted to opioids."

"Oh, Chance." My chest tightened with sympathy and shock. "I can't imagine what you went through."

He nodded once, still without looking at me. "Do you want a salad with your pasta?"

Message received. Off-limits topic.

"Please. Can I help with something?"

"You sit. I got this."

I tried to remember the last time someone had cooked for me, cared for me. Gram, sure, but it'd been years since she'd been able. Guys? No one came to mind. I'd had lots of short-term relationships. Christian was the only one I'd thought was more serious at the time. None of them had cooked for me.

Not that this was a relationship. Just a kind gesture. Or maybe just what he'd said—a way for us to talk in private.

"So you wanted to talk," I prompted, thinking a lunch hour was hardly enough time to cover the complexity of our situation.

"Yeah." He began slicing chicken into bite-sized pieces on a cutting board. "I stand by what I said Friday, Rowan." He paused and looked at me. "I'm in this. We share responsibility for what happened, and that responsibility is a life-long thing. Not just financially. I don't know how we'll make it work, but this child will have me in his or her life."

"That's important," I said cautiously.

"You sound like you don't believe me."

I sorted through my thoughts and searched for the right words. Careful but sure words. "Your involvement is welcome, as long as you don't have any ideas about taking this child away from me or trying to get full-time custody."

He set down his knife and faced me again. "Have I given you the impression I'd do that to you?" He looked genuinely confused and maybe even...hurt?

"No. You seem like a good man determined to fulfill your responsibilities as a father. I just needed to be sure we understand each other. I'm the baby's mother. I'm in a vulnerable position, trying to get back on my feet, but I *will* be back on my feet. This baby is everything to me."

Chance turned back to the food, dumping the chicken into a hot pan. "A child needs her mother," he said with conviction. "I know this firsthand. I'm hoping we'll be able to work as a team somehow. Being the only parent..." He shook his head. "Zero stars. Two thumbs down. I don't recommend it. What that'll look like for us? I have no idea, but all I meant to say was that I'll be part of it. An active parent."

I relaxed a little. "Okay."

"Are you planning to stay in Dragonfly Lake long-term?"

"My career will dictate that to some extent. If I could get a position at the high school..." This fall was likely out, but next year I'd be ready to get back in the classroom. "I'm starting to love the town. I'd like to make it work."

"This place is like that. It left an impression on me when I was a kid. I came back." He busied himself prepping a salad while the chicken cooked. "That's a long-term concern. More pressing is how we'll handle work and town gossip. We'll need to level with Holden and Chloe."

"Of course."

"Which means it'll become common knowledge. Which means we'll have our day on the gossip train. Can you handle that?"

I shrugged. "It is what it is. We had a fling. I won't apologize for it."

With a smile, he looked at me and said, "I like your guts."

"We should tell our bosses sooner rather than later."

"I agree, but first..."

"Your daughter," I guessed.

"Yeah," he said on an exhale. "That's not going to be fun."

"It's a firsthand lesson on the odds of getting pregnant," I said sympathetically.

"It is that. I haven't had any relationships since her mother died. So she'll have to face that her dad had sex, as well as the prospect of becoming a half sister."

"That's a lot to swallow at fourteen."

"I don't want her to hear it from someone else."

"That would be bad."

"I need some time to figure out how to break it to her."

"I won't be showing for several weeks."

"You'll sign up for health insurance right away?" He put precooked pasta in the microwave.

"Already done."

Again he met my gaze. "Thank you."

"It's a relief," I told him. "I never intended to not have insurance, but when my Gram was no longer able to be by herself, my life kind of blew up."

My stomach gurgled with uneasiness as Chance set a

large salad in front of me then followed it with a plate of steaming chicken and pasta. I wasn't sure if it was the food or the emotions that aroused the hint of nausea.

"She was lucky to have you," he said as he took the stool next to me and pulled his own plate close.

I felt that oh-so-familiar swelling in my throat. "I was lucky to have her first." I shoved a bite of salad in my mouth to give myself a few seconds. As I chewed, I battled down the fresh wave of emotions. By the time I swallowed, I could say more without my voice wavering. "She took me in when my parents died."

"You said they were in an accident?"

"They'd saved up for the honeymoon of their dreams. It'd been seven years since they got married. They finally got to go to Hawaii. They went on one of those helicopter tours of the islands, and their helicopter crashed."

"Jesus. That's awful." He took another bite and chewed. Eventually he said, "Losing a parent is damn hard no matter how old you are. Both at once?" He shook his head. "I can't imagine."

"Did you lose yours?"

"No. They live in Missouri. We're not close. But Sam... I've seen what losing her mom did to her. I sometimes wonder if she'd be less...lost if her mom was still alive."

"That's hard to say. Impossible to prove," I said. "Teenagers are dealing with so much even if they have a solid family life."

"I know that. I just wonder how I can do better, be more for her. Kissing her boo-boos when she was little was one thing. Filling in for her mother now?" He shook his head. "I'm fucking drowning."

As we ate, he told me about Sam's friend struggles and how he'd found her at the beach with boys and alcohol.

"Those 'friends' dumped her," he said between bites of chicken.

"Let me guess," I said. "You're torn between being pissed at the kids for hurting your daughter and relieved she's no longer friends with them."

"That sums it up. She stayed home all weekend. She seems sad. The only good thing is that she let me comfort her Thursday night. That hasn't happened for months."

"Those kids weren't the right ones for her."

"I know that, and you know that," he said.

"She probably knows it too."

He nodded and shoved his empty plate and bowl away. I did the same, though I'd only eaten half of it.

"You're not hungry?" he asked. "Or you didn't like it?"

"I liked it," I said in a rush. "It was really good, but my stomach is wobbly lately."

"Morning sickness?"

"Morning sickness, yes. Smell-of-food sickness, yes. It comes and goes throughout the day. The heavier the food, the more likely it is to bring on nausea."

"My wife had the round-the-clock nausea," he said sympathetically. "The upside is that it's a sign of a healthy pregnancy."

I'd read that too. "I appreciate you cooking for me. It really was tasty...until that flip of the stomach."

Chance stood, went around the counter to the sink, and rinsed off both plates. He placed them in the dishwasher as I drank the rest of my water.

"Come with me," he said. I must've given him a puzzled look, because he added, "I'll show you around."

The main floor had two steps down to a family room, plus a half bath, a formal living room, and a dining room he'd turned into an office.

Following him up the stairs to the second level, I felt weird. Like, why did I need to see the private parts of his house? But I couldn't deny—to myself only—I was curious to lay eyes on his bedroom.

He showed me his room first, just opened the door to the master and allowed me a peek in, as if that was *not* his objective, but I couldn't figure out what was.

My too-short glance in showed me dark gray walls, lots of wood, and creams and grays for the bedding. It was masculine but cozy. I wouldn't mind getting wrapped up in those sheets.

Stop it, Rowan.

I darted my gaze away as if I hadn't given any extra thought to the place he slept. Did he sleep naked?

No, no, no.

The temperature seemed to climb, and my face felt flushed.

"Sam used to have this room," he said, leading me past a bathroom to the other side of the stairway, where there were two doors. Sam's was the one directly across from his room, but it was mostly empty. "The basement is her kingdom now, which might be a mistake. I don't know. Who the hell ever knows? Parenting is a mind fuck."

"Sign me right up for that, please," I said dryly.

He grinned. "Fasten your seat belt."

He ran his hand down my back in a brief but intimate touch. I pretended not to notice, but oh, did I notice.

"This is the infrequently used guest room." He opened the door to the last bedroom.

Inside was a comfortable-looking room with a queen bed, a nightstand, a window seat, and a dresser along one wall. The bed was covered by a thick navy-blue comforter and multiple pillows.

"Your infrequent guests are lucky," I said, thinking there was nothing about his house that screamed bachelor pad. It was homey with more of a family feel.

"I'm glad you think so. I know you're looking for a place to live. We've got plenty of space here, so...would you like to move in?"

Chapter Fourteen

Rowan

I was turning away from the door of the guest room, an empty smile on my face, when Chance's words sank in.

With a glance at him, I tried to decipher his intent.

Move in?

Here?

Was he making a move? Like, wanting to be a couple? A living-together couple?

No. Of course not.

He was being kind. Generous. A good guy. We hardly knew each other. We didn't have a true friendship, let alone a relationship, unless you counted that, oh, *he was my boss*.

"We can't do that," I said. "I can't move in with my boss."

A grin crawled across his features. "I'm not your boss."

"You kind of are."

"Chloe's your boss."

"You're the boss of marketing things, and apparently I have to do marketing things."

His smile faded. "You don't want to do marketing?"

"It's fine, Chance. That's not the point here."

"Right. The point is that you need a place to live. I have lots of room."

I tried to think of the shit ton of ramifications living here would have. His daughter. Our coworkers. The town gossip train. *Us.*

No, not us. We weren't an *us.*

"That sounds like it could cause all kinds of problems," I said.

He let out a sardonic chuckle. "You mean more problems than having a baby together after a one-night fling in a small town will cause?"

I had to laugh along with him. If I didn't, I'd cry. "Good point. But what's your daughter going to say?"

"I'd like to think she would be on board with helping out one of my coworkers."

"Or your underlings," I said.

"Rowan, stop. Rusty Anchor isn't like that. It's too small. We're more like a work family than a corporation with a strict hierarchy."

"I know," I allowed.

I tried to imagine sleeping across the hall from this man. This man who taunted my thoughts, as it was, when I was sleeping alone in my safe little room at the inn.

"How would that work exactly?" I asked.

"You'd move your belongings into this room"—he slapped the doorframe—"and anywhere else you want. I don't know. You can hole up in your room if you want to, or you can make yourself at home in the rest of the house. It's a big house for three people."

I frowned as I thought through the idea. Would I ever feel comfortable curling up in his living room to read a book? Bingeing reality TV in his family room? Cooking my dinner in his kitchen?

"I'm looking at a place tomorrow," I told him.

"What place?"

"It's a garage apartment on"—I pulled my phone out to look up the street name—"Cherry Street."

"Let's talk more while I clean up the kitchen."

"I'll help." I was determined to, even though my stomach was still uneasy.

We went back downstairs, my gaze taking in everything as I imagined what it would be like to live here. The house itself was cozy, comfy, well-kept, and clean. The place wasn't the issue.

The issue was the man. My attraction to him. Well, that and a jillion other details.

Would living in the same house, seeing his human side —the side that left socks on the floor or sang off-key in the shower or whatever his annoying habits were—would that snuff out the sparks of attraction? Or would it intensify them?

"A garage apartment, huh?" Chance asked as he tidied the kitchen counter.

"It's small, but it would be just me."

"Then you and a baby."

I started washing one of the pans. "Right. How would that work here though? A baby will shake up everything. I can be a quiet, invisible roommate until the baby's born."

"You won't have to be quiet or invisible here."

"Sam might think otherwise."

"Sam doesn't pay the mortgage."

"But she's your daughter. I don't want to do anything to cause trouble between you two."

He let out a hollow laugh. "Oh, I think that ship sailed when I got you pregnant. She's going to have a hard time with that. But that's on me to navigate."

"She's going to hate me as soon as she finds out the truth," I said.

"I'd like to think we'll help her work through that. At any rate, Sam will have a lot to process whether you're living here or not. If you're living here, she can get to know you."

Part of me really wanted to meet his daughter, but another part was terrified.

I'd handled teenagers all the time as a teacher. I could usually develop a good rapport, even with some of the harder cases. But the stakes were high here. Sam would be my baby's half sibling. I didn't know how big Chance's extended family was, but mine was nonexistent. I didn't want to ruin their chances for a sibling relationship even before the baby's birth.

Chance took the clean pan from me and dried it.

"What happens when the baby's born?" I asked.

"Then we parent him or her together."

"And I just...live here?" I shook my head. Our situation seemed more and more outrageous the further into the future I considered.

Chance shrugged as if it wasn't a big deal. "For as long as you want to."

"I want my own house." Particularly if he ever got involved with someone new. The thought of him going on dates, falling in love... A pang of jealousy hit me. I didn't want to witness any of that.

"Then you can get your own house when you're ready.

If you live here now, rent will be cheap, and you can save money."

"How cheap?" I asked, thinking of that insurance premium I'd committed to.

"A couple hundred a month."

"Stop. That's not rent."

"It's my house. I can pay the mortgage just fine. You're trying to get back on your feet."

"There's a fine line between getting back on my feet and being a charity case."

He set the dry pan down hard on the counter and turned to me. "Rowan. You're carrying my child. I want to do whatever I can to support you. That's not charity. It's in my best interests—and the baby's—that you're in a safe, healthy place."

I could see his point when he said it like that, but two hundred dollars?

Rent that low would be a godsend for sure.

But there was that downside. That proximity to Chance. Kind, sexy, way-too-tempting Chance.

"Let me think about it for a few days," I said as I finished washing the second pan. "I'll go through the garage apartment tomorrow and keep checking for new listings."

"Whatever you need to do. Just know the offer stands."

As I handed the pan to him, I turned to face him, met his handsome gaze, and said, "Okay," on an exhalation. "Options are good. Thank you."

I needed to make this decision based on logic, after weighing my options carefully, not on emotions or attraction. My baby was depending on me to be smart about every decision I made from here on out.

No pressure. No pressure at all.

Chapter Fifteen

Rowan

I should've known, when the owner of the garage apartment postponed my tour of it for two days, it wasn't going to work out.

It turned out she'd postponed because the sink had leaked everywhere, and she'd needed to clean it and let it dry.

Points for her for leveling with me, but there were multiple reasons I couldn't raise my baby in that studio apartment, not even for a few weeks.

After my tour, I parked in the Rusty Anchor lot and sat in my car while I gulped down the rest of my PB-and-J lunch. As I ate, I pulled up the Tattler app again to see if there were any new listings since last night. Of course there weren't. I did an internet search for rentals in Dragonfly Lake, but again, no miracles popped up.

When my sandwich was gone, I headed inside to get back to work. I was sick of worrying about my living situation. My afternoon work tasks would be a welcome distraction.

After throwing my coat and hat into my office, I grabbed the box of promotional materials from my table and went out to the second-floor public area so I could spread out and work faster.

Kemp had developed two special beers with a Valentine's focus: Dark Desire, a chocolate stout, and a cherry wheat called Love Is the Pits. Not only did we have a fancy Valentine's evening soiree to celebrate them, but Henry's Restaurant would be pushing them hard throughout the month of February. I'd picked up the materials from the printer this morning, and now I needed to assemble the table toppers, prep the menu inserts, and take some photos of the two brews for social media.

I was halfway through the table toppers when I heard footsteps behind me.

"How's it going?" Chance asked. Even though I'd suspected it was him, my heart tripped up at the sound of his voice.

"Good," I said automatically, folding another topper and assembling it.

He picked up one of the table tents and looked at both sides, then nodded. He'd inspected them earlier today, so that wasn't why he was here.

He sat on a stool at the table where I was working. I glanced up at him and smiled as I would at any of my coworkers. Damn if I didn't get a jolt from how good-looking he was, just like I always did. I did my best to ignore the stupid reaction.

"How was the apartment?" he asked.

That was the real reason he'd come out.

I merely shook my head as images of the mildewy place filled my mind.

"Not good?"

"It was bad. Now I know why the rent is in my budget." I put the topper on the adjacent table with the others and started on the next one. "It was old, drafty, and had enough water damage that I wouldn't sleep there myself, let alone bring a baby in."

"I'm sorry. I know you were hoping it would work."

I looked up at him. "It's nothing against you. Just...I was hoping to have my own space."

"You'd have your own space in my house. Your room would be your castle." He smiled and kept his tone light, but I didn't feel light.

I felt trapped.

Chance glanced over his shoulder as if checking that we were alone. I knew we were. The acoustics of this room made it impossible to sneak in.

"Why are you fighting this so hard, Rowan? Help me understand."

My emotions jumbled up in my throat, making it hard to speak. I didn't want to get emotional, not over this. I spent so much of my time feeling overwrought and overwhelmed by feelings these days.

The baby alone was so much to absorb. Parenthood? Me? Right now? Who thought I was capable of being responsible for a child? I often felt like a child myself, particularly since all the people who'd raised me were now gone. If Gram were alive, I'd be so much more confident becoming a mom. She would've guided me through.

Grief seeped through cracks in the floodwall as it did multiple times a day, often when I least expected it. I steeled myself, patching up the crevasses, hoping they'd hold until I was alone at the inn tonight.

When I thought I could talk without crying, I kept my eyes on yet another topper, folding, assembling, fastening.

How much could I admit to him?

I trusted him with a lot. Maybe it was myself I didn't trust enough.

Probably it was myself.

"You know I'm vulnerable right now. And by vulnerable, I mean an emotional train wreck." I managed an upward tilt of my lips.

"Of course you are," he said. His voice held compassion, understanding.

Focusing my gaze on the next topper, I continued, "I need to get my feet under me, Chance. Caring for my grandmother"—my voice wavered but I pushed through it—"I wouldn't trade my time with her for anything. It was an extraordinary privilege to be the person she trusted to see her out of this realm. That probably sounds weird..." I shook my head, unable to explain any better what I felt from the depths of my soul.

"Not weird. I've never been in that position, but I sort of understand."

I nodded, content with that. Relieved he didn't make a face like I was nuts or ask me to explain it. "Anyway, it... took a lot out of me. I basically set myself aside to take care of her. Myself, my needs, my everything. Out of necessity. I don't want sympathy," I said in a rush. "Like I said, I chose to be there for her, and I'd make the same choice again."

"I understand that, Rowan. I meant it when I said she was lucky to have you."

I ignored that, determined to get the rest of my thoughts

out in answer to his original question. "To get pregnant now..." I pressed my lips together and shook my head.

"Irony is a bitch, isn't it?" He smiled as he said it, and I grinned too because, well, that was the truth, and I knew becoming a father again hadn't been on his to-do list. Once again, if I didn't laugh, I'd cry.

I was so tired of crying.

"You're being amazing, Chance, and that's part of the problem."

He reared back, as if that wasn't where he thought I'd go. "Explain that?"

I smiled to soften my answer. "You're supportive and understanding." *Not to mention so damn good-looking.* "You cooked me lunch, offered me a cheap place to stay. You ask how I'm feeling. You seem like the kind of guy who'd hold back a girl's hair when she gets sick."

His amused grin made me suspect he'd done that very thing at some point in his life.

"And I appreciate all of it," I said. "But I'm also scared I'll get too used to it."

"So you'll move in if I'm mean to you?" His dimple appeared.

I laughed lightly. "Please no. I appreciate your kindness."

I set the assembled topper down. God help me, how did I say what I needed to say without saying exactly what I was afraid of—that I'd drift into a relationship with him because it was convenient and tempting to be cared for? I didn't trust myself to make wise decisions for my own future right now.

"We're already straddling this awkward connection of working together and expecting a baby," I said quietly.

He nodded.

"If we live together, it's going to get even messier." I tapped my index finger on the table, searching for the right words. "Harder for me to stay clear-minded and make good decisions."

"We'll make decisions together," he said.

"For the baby, yes."

He studied me for several seconds, making me antsy. I picked up another topper and folded it.

"You don't want more between us than co-parenting," he finally guessed.

"Yes. Exactly."

"We already agreed to that."

I laughed dryly. "Chance. That coworkers-only thing was before there was a baby or living together in the mix."

Understanding washed over his features. "Right. So you're afraid the lines would be blurrier."

"Aren't you?"

"We'll be going in with our eyes open. As long as we communicate, we'll be fine. You're not open to anything deeper, and neither am I. Nothing's changed."

"It would be easy for me to imagine there's more between us than there is," I finally said. "Because I'm a hot mess right now."

"I wouldn't take advantage of you."

"I know." I closed my eyes, because looking at this gorgeous man was *not* making it easier to make my point. "It's me, Chance. Weak link." I raised my hand. "I don't want to learn to rely on you. I don't want to develop feelings for you just because you're amazing and I'm going through some things."

After a moment, he sat up straighter and puffed out his chest. "You think I'm amazing?" A boyish grin stole over his face, and *God*.

That.

That look, that charm...*that* was trouble.

"Stop it," I said, grinning in spite of myself.

"You said I'm amazing."

"I might have overstated. How about, you're not a douche."

Chance threw his head back and laughed. "I want that on my tombstone. 'He wasn't a douche.'"

I screwed up my face. "Who wants a tombstone these days? Real estate is limited."

"You have a point." He laughed again then sobered. "Rowan, I'm still getting to know you, but from what I've seen, you've got an inner strength that'll get you through, with or without me."

Something in his words got through my thick skull and penetrated my gray matter. I knew it took a strong person to care for a loved one through dementia. It had tested me every day, was the absolute hardest thing I'd ever been through, but I'd made it. I liked to think I'd learned to be strong from my Gram.

She'd withstood the loss of an adult child. She'd stepped in to raise me when she was beyond child-rearing years and should've been enjoying a carefree empty nest. She'd weathered the death of her lifelong love in my grandfather. She'd grieved. Of course she'd grieved both her husband and her daughter. But she'd faced life with a quiet, tangible determination to make the most of what she still had.

If I said yes to moving in with Chance, I'd be going in with my eyes wide-open as he said. My guard up. I wasn't stupid, and I wasn't weak, thanks to the woman who'd raised me. I wouldn't let myself *drift* into anything that wouldn't be good for me or the baby.

I nodded, thinking it through, reasoning with myself.

"Okay." I drew in a deep, steady breath. "Okay. Yes, I'll take you up on your generous offer on that spare bedroom. Thank you, Chance."

A gorgeous smile broke out across his lips, almost making me retract my acceptance, until he said, "I'll try to be a little less amazing."

Laughing, I said, "Don't you dare."

Inside, I braced myself. Erected my walls a little higher. And told myself—over and over—I could resist my charming, kind-hearted baby daddy.

Chapter Sixteen

Chance

My nerves were stretched to the limit Saturday afternoon as I paced from the kitchen to my home office window and back. Again and again. Watching for Rowan's car.

She was checking out of the inn today and moving into our spare bedroom. Checkout was hours ago, but she'd told me she had errands to run before she came over.

I couldn't imagine what errands could take this long, but I recognized that was none of my business.

Still, the anticipation of...*everything* was making me want to crawl out of my skin.

At the top of the list was Sam. She and Rowan hadn't met yet. We hadn't been able to arrange it in the two days since Rowan had agreed to move in.

When I'd told Sam about our new roommate, she'd been quiet, nodded, but had not really given a hint of her thoughts. She just seemed...sad. She didn't know about New Year's Eve, the pregnancy, nothing except that Rowan was new to town, worked at the brewery, and needed a place to live.

I was worried that adding Rowan to our household would push my daughter even further away, but I stood by my decision. Rowan had no one. No support. I was determined to be there for both Rowan and Sam.

I went to the family room, forced my nervous ass down on the sofa, and pulled out my phone to pass the time. I had ebooks I could read. A few game apps. The entire internet.

None of it could distract me.

As hard as I tried to stay put, I popped up seconds later, paced up the two stairs to the kitchen level, trooped through my office, and peered out the blinds.

And there she was, pulling into the driveway.

I headed to the garage and hit the opener. Her arrival would be less public if she parked in the garage, but I reminded myself we weren't going for private. She was moving in. It would not be a secret.

Her pregnancy... That was a different story for now. We hoped to control *when* that secret came out.

As Rowan killed the engine, I walked to the driver's side door.

"Welcome," I said when she opened it. I didn't have to fake my smile at the sight of her.

She looked harried but beautiful in her lavender puffer coat, her chestnut hair tousled beneath her gray stocking cap with a big, furry ball at the tip. Her cheeks were pink, her brown eyes tired but pretty as she climbed out.

"Thank you."

I glanced at her backseat, expecting it to be overflowing with her belongings. There was a box, some pillows, and an overstuffed bag.

"That's not very much stuff," I said.

"The trunk's pretty full."

The trunk wouldn't hold a lot, but then she'd warned me she wouldn't take up much room in my house.

I opened the back door, prepared to carry her things inside, but Rowan stopped me with a hand on my arm.

"I want to meet Sam first," she said.

"You can absolutely meet her. We might as well take a load in while we go."

She squeezed my arm again and shook her head. "Not yet. Please?"

Confused, I tried to read her expression. She bit her lower lip and glanced toward the house.

"Sam first," she said. "Empty-handed. I'd rather not look like I'm here to invade her territory by lugging my crap in."

I straightened and studied her.

"I don't want to put her on the defensive," she continued. "This is her home. She's your *daughter*, Chance. This first meeting is important."

She was right, and I hadn't thought of any of that.

I nodded, feeling like the worst dad ever. I'd been uptight about Rowan arriving, about her meeting my daughter, and still, I hadn't come up with ways to make it easier for Sam.

My appreciation for this woman grew every day. Surface things had drawn me to her on New Year's Eve— her looks, an expression in her eyes, her smile—but the deeper I got to know her, the more I liked her.

I was awed by her determination to be independent and to get back on her feet after what she'd been through with her grandmother. She'd jumped into a job where she had no relevant experience and, from what I'd seen so far, learned fast, figured out a lot on her own, and asked questions when she needed to. She was easy to get along with, likable, and now she was determined to win my daughter over.

Pulling myself out of my thoughts, I walked beside her through the garage, my hand on her waist without thinking about it.

Once in the kitchen, I glanced at the door to the basement and felt like I needed to warn Rowan.

"Sam might not be friendly," I said in a low voice. "I'll apologize in advance in case she's rude. I didn't raise her to be rude but—"

"She's fourteen. I understand. I'm the intruder here, Chance. And I'm a big girl. I can handle a little teenage rejection." She smiled, but I could see through it to her nervousness.

I took her hand and squeezed it. "Here goes nothing."

I opened the basement door, called my daughter, and got no reply. Pulling out my phone, I texted her, all too used to having to communicate this way because she existed with her earbuds on. One day they were going to fuse with her ears.

I shot an apologetic look to Rowan, but she merely shrugged as if she wasn't fazed. When her gaze flickered away, though, I caught another glimpse of insecurity. For a moment, I had the urge to pull her into my arms and assure her it would be fine, but I shoved one hand into my pocket to stop myself. Wouldn't that be awkward.

Sam took her sweet time, but she eventually appeared, wearing leggings, a cropped tank, an oversized black-and-white cardigan, and a frown. Her long hair hung down her back.

"Hey, Sam, this is Rowan. Rowan, my daughter."

"Hi, Sam." Rowan extended a hand, which my

daughter shook. "I'm glad to meet you finally. I like your sweater."

"Oh. Thanks," Sam said, sounding surprised as she glanced down at her clothing. When she looked back up, there was a shy smile on her face. "Cute jacket. I want one like that but in white."

"I considered white," Rowan said with an *OMG-me-too* tone. "I figured I would get it dirty in less than a day."

I looked between them, a little stunned. I'd been so worried my daughter wouldn't give Rowan a chance, but twenty seconds in and they were bonding over clothes?

And here I'd been frowning because I could see my daughter's navel. No dad wanted his daughter showing off too much skin, did he?

The two of them discussed where Rowan had bought it —Lake Girl Boutique here in town—and other color choices as I stood there mute, puzzled by this instant connection. This immediate female common ground.

Once that topic was exhausted, Rowan said, "I know it's been just you and your dad here for a long time, so it'll be weird to have someone else in your house. I'll try to stay out of your way."

"You won't be in my way," Sam said. "I mostly stay in the basement."

"Well, I appreciate you and your dad opening your home to me. I really like this town so far, but it's impossible to find an apartment."

"We've got plenty of room," I said. "Make yourself at home and let us know if you need anything, right, Sam?"

My daughter shot me a glance then said, "Sure. I'm gonna go back downstairs."

"Nice to meet you," Rowan said.

Sam paused. "Yeah. You too." My daughter smiled, just

a faint tilting upward of her lips, but it hit me that it'd been a damn long time since I'd seen her smile.

Once Sam was back in the basement, I stood there trying to process the past five minutes. "That went better than I expected."

"She seems sweet," Rowan said.

"She is." Even if I hadn't seen her sweet side for ages before today. Shaking my head, I said, "Let's get you moved in."

We had her car empty in three trips. As I set her biggest suitcase on the floor of her room, I took in the short stacks on the floor along the wall, where we'd placed everything else. My brows shot up. "This is really all you brought?"

Rowan nodded. "Everything I own. When I cleaned out my grandmother's house, I knew I couldn't take a bunch of useless stuff with me, so I was pretty ruthless getting rid of things."

There were two suitcases, a few boxes, a duffel bag, a couple of totes... It didn't seem like much at all.

"I was in crisis mode for like two years straight," she said quietly. "My perspective changed. I gave up all my classroom supplies, which I might regret eventually, but I can't imagine lugging them around now. I lost enough weight from stress that half my clothes didn't fit anymore, so I donated them. I've got my favorite books, a box of photos and memories from my childhood, my toiletries and jewelry." She shrugged as if to say, *what more could a girl need?* "Oh, and pillows. I'm super picky about pillows." She laughed self-consciously.

"You've lost a lot, haven't you?"

She swallowed and attempted a smile. "The only loss that matters is my Gram. The rest is just stuff."

For the second time today, I itched to pull her into my

arms. I wanted to reassure her, but I didn't have the right to do that.

It wasn't pity I felt for her but empathy. Loss was a bitch, but I sensed it was just the tip of what she'd been through. Watching someone you loved fail one day at a time... I'd done that with Erin in a lot of ways. I'd known my wife had a problem with pills. I could see her decline more clearly in hindsight. At the time, I hadn't realized how far into addiction she was or how she'd been fading day by day.

Addiction and dementia were not the same thing though. They were different flavors of heartbreak. I'd had years to work through mine and come out on the other side. Rowan was just getting started.

She turned in a circle, taking in her new room, and when she faced me again, there was so much raw emotion in her expression. "Thank you, Chance. I don't know what I would've done if you hadn't opened your home to me." She blinked, and a tear plummeted down her cheek. She swiped it away in a hurry.

Dammit. To hell with awkward.

"Can I hug you? As a friend? You look like you need it." She hesitated, then nodded.

I stepped forward and enfolded her in my arms. She wrapped her arms around me and leaned her head against my chest. Relaxing into her touch, only then did I realize how much I'd been yearning to feel her in my arms again. There was a rightness to it that didn't make sense. Maybe it stemmed from the fact that we shared such a big, intimate secret and yet were unable to show any kind of ties other than professional ones at work. That took effort. Caused a strain. And now, finally, the strain was gone.

"This is your home for as long as you need it," I said.

She sniffled, then laughed quietly, her head still resting

on me. "I'm sorry. These are tears of gratitude, not sadness. Pregnancy hormones are no joke. I cried during a stupid TV commercial the other day."

"Cry all you need to," I said, grinning with her.

As I breathed in her floral scent, there was a stirring in my body, a reaction below the waist that had me putting a little space between us. The intent of the hug wasn't to get a cheap thrill. I didn't want to put her off or raise her guard. My objective was to be there for her, support her, be a friend.

Though I would never say Rowan was fragile—from what I'd seen, she had a quiet, determined thread of steel inside of her—she needed care and friendship right now, not some dude with a hard-on. I'd invited her to live here with the intention of providing something she needed—shelter and support.

I ended the hug. No need to make things weird on the first day.

"You're welcome to use the kitchen anytime you want, to make whatever you want, but tonight, I'm treating to carryout from Henry's."

"I love Henry's. But I can pay for my own."

"Not tonight, Rowan. It's your welcome dinner, and I'm not taking your money."

She grinned. "I didn't realize you have a bossy side. I guess it's fitting since you're my boss."

"I'm not your boss." I shook my head but couldn't help smiling back, knowing she threw that line at me just to get under my skin. "Let me know what you want before dinnertime."

"I will. Thanks."

"You need any help unpacking?"

She glanced at her belongings and shook her head. "It's

mostly just my clothes. A lot of the other stuff will stay in boxes."

"I'll leave you to it then." I headed toward the door, stopped when I reached it, and looked at her. "Make yourself at home. I'm glad you're here."

She met my gaze, appearing startled at my admission, then said, "Me too."

Chapter Seventeen

Rowan

Monday morning, it was a relief to go to work.

Living with Chance was...tricky.

He was a charming, thoughtful host, making me feel welcome while giving me space, but it'd been a long time since I'd had a roommate besides Gram. Living with a man and his teenage daughter was different enough, even when you didn't consider that I'd slept with said man once, was carrying his child, and still found him incredibly attractive.

It was going to take some time for me to be able to fully relax and feel at home, if that was even possible. Because I needed to keep my guard up against that attraction.

I was in a vulnerable spot. I could fully own that my emotions were a nonstop churning storm. Not only was I grieving the woman who'd raised me, but I was adjusting to the idea of motherhood, straddling the line between caution and hope. Caution because my pregnancy was high-risk. The truth was, I was terrified something would go wrong. I was scared to nurture those hopes about holding my own child in my arms.

In other words, I was a hot mess even before adding living with the sexy, off-limits father of my baby.

So yeah... Work would be a break, at least when I wasn't working directly with Chance.

This morning, I had a meeting with Chloe. When it was time, I picked up my notebook and headed toward her office, thankful Chance's door was closed as I passed.

As I reached Chloe's open door, she was setting her cell phone down.

"Hey, come on in," she said, standing from her desk.

"Welcome back," I said. "How's Sutton?"

Chloe had stayed home for several days last week because her daughter was sick.

"She's well and back at Quincy's today. I just hung up with Presley. Have you talked to her? They finally came to an agreement. She got the house."

"That took a while," I said. From what I understood, there'd been a lot of back-and-forth. "She must be super excited. Has she figured out her plans for her new little purchase?" I laughed as I said it because the house our friend had bought—with cash—was not at all little.

"Of course not, but that's our Presley. Buy a house on a whim. Figure out what to do with it later."

"Gotta love her," I said, meaning it.

"She mentioned the possibility of gutting it."

"I can't wait to see it."

Chloe closed the door as I headed to her table, where we usually met. "It's warmer in here when I close the door," she said. Then she paused and her brows went up. "Or have you hit that point in the pregnancy when you're hot all the time?"

"No," I answered. "That will probably start just as it gets stupid hot outside."

With a grin she said, "Most likely. How are you feeling?" She set her laptop on the table and sat next to me.

"Mostly okay. Every once in a while food makes me feel sick, but I've only thrown up a couple of times."

"I hope that gets better instead of worse," she said.

"Same. The fatigue is real though."

She'd warned me about it early on. Between being pregnant, moving, and wrestling with the shit storm of emotional stuff, I was ready to collapse in bed by dinnertime each evening.

"I remember how bad it was during the first trimester," Chloe said. "Did you extend your stay at the inn? Ava said she'd give you the same rate break, right?"

"Yeah. And no. Ava's a doll, but I found a cheaper solution." Even with the rate break, the inn was a lot for my puny budget.

"Oh, good. What'd you find?"

"I found a room for rent in a house." I swallowed, preparing for her reaction. "In Chance's house."

"Our Chance?"

"The one and only. Sam's room is in the basement, and he has two extra bedrooms upstairs."

I could see her mind chewing on that as she nodded. "I didn't realize you two were that cozy."

"We're not cozy," I said with a nervous laugh.

I was pulled in three directions as I tried to decide how much to tell her.

Chloe was my boss and my friend, and those each called for differing levels of info. On top of that, Chance and I had agreed not to spread the word about the baby until we'd told Sam.

Leaning forward, I planted my elbows on the table and ran my hands over my face tiredly, debating.

Chloe and Presley were my confidantes. They knew a lot of the details about my pregnancy, but not about the father. They'd been respectful of my desire to keep his name to myself.

But I was dying to talk to someone, another female who could relate and help me navigate this muddled situation.

Most importantly, I trusted Chloe to keep our secret.

I eyed the door to make sure it was closed all the way and said quietly, "I need to tell you some things, but they involve other people, so—"

"This is confidential," she said. "Got it. I'll keep it to myself."

I pressed my lips together and summoned my courage. "Chance is the father," I said in a hushed voice.

Chloe sucked in a breath, her brows popping upward again. She stared at me with her mouth gaping for several seconds.

I nodded.

She covered her mouth with both hands and continued to watch me.

"He was my New Year's kiss guy," I said simply. "Except there was more."

Chloe's grin stretched across her face as she lowered her hands. "I had no idea. And then you started working here..."

"We didn't talk about where he worked that night. He said he was in marketing. I told him I was a teacher. We, um, didn't spend too much time on our life stories."

"I'm betting not," she said with a laugh. "Wow. So you didn't know he worked here until your first day?"

"We didn't exchange contact info. We had no reason to. So yeah, on my first day of work, there he suddenly was."

Chloe looked to be taking everything in. "And then you found out you're pregnant. What's the *chance* of that? Pun is totally intended."

I smiled. "I'm sorry I didn't tell you sooner—"

"I get it. You had to tell him. And then there's Sam..."

"She doesn't know yet. That's why I swore you to secrecy."

"Oh, Rowan." She reached over the table and took my hand. "This is a lot for you to handle."

"Which is why I spilled it all today. Because *I'm living in his house.*" I whispered the last part, fully aware of Chance's office on the other side of the wall.

"Are you two...involved?" she asked, as if the possibility had just occurred to her.

"It was just a fling. Neither of us is up for entanglements."

"I'd say a baby is an entanglement."

"Understatement. But you know what I mean."

"Wow. If ever you needed a girls' night..."

"Amen."

"You're okay living there though?"

I nodded. "He's been great so far."

"So he's supportive of the baby?"

I expelled a heavy breath. "He says he wants to co-parent. We haven't defined what that looks like yet."

Chloe's expression softened. "He has a big heart." She tilted her head. "So is he going to your appointment with you this week?"

I'd emailed her about my upcoming ultrasound, but I hadn't thought to mention it to Chance. "Uh, I have no idea." I leaned back and closed my eyes. "I guess I should ask?"

"If it's an ultrasound..." Chloe nodded as I opened my eyes. "Those are pretty amazing."

I swallowed hard, keeping my fears about what we'd discover to myself. If it was bad news, I wouldn't want to be alone.

"I guess I better ask him," I said. "And apologize to you and Holden for pulling two of us out of work."

"No need to apologize." She frowned. "Holden will have to know soon."

I nodded. "You can share with him as long as—"

"He'll keep it to himself."

"Thanks, Chloe."

"Of course. You, me, and Presley are doing girls' night soon. With mocktails."

"Yes, please."

"I suppose we should get down to work. Oh, God, and I just asked you to work closely with Chance."

A laugh bubbled out of me. "And I couldn't say anything."

She sobered. "Is it a problem for you?"

"It's fine. Comical, really. But he's been super patient with my lack of marketing background."

She studied me for a few seconds. "You two work well together?"

"We do."

Now she sat back, looking thoughtful.

"Professionally. We're not..." I shook my head. "We're just not, personally. I mean it, Chloe."

"Chance is solid." She lowered her voice. "And not hard to look at."

"That's what got me into trouble in the first place." I laughed, then went serious. "I can't do it. It would be too easy to fall into something just because it's easy. I have no business being in a relationship right now, not that he's asked me to be. I don't want to drift into something because it's convenient and I'm tired. Like, life tired, you know? And he's there to make it easier."

"That's smart."

"With this baby on the way, I need to make smart, strong, clear-minded decisions. Not be lured in by a good-looking guy who's in a different stage of his life."

She nodded. "I think you've got your head on straighter than you might think, but it's good to be cautious." She checked the time on her phone. "I have an appointment in forty minutes, so we should get to business."

"Yes to business," I said, relieved in multiple ways. Keeping the truth from Chloe had been weighing on me. "Because apparently I need to ask the father of my baby to the ultrasound as soon as we're done here."

I had no idea which answer I wanted more, a yes or a no.

Chapter Eighteen

Rowan

A no would've been less awkward.

True to form, though, Chance was only too willing to come to the ultrasound with me later that week, so now we were trapped in a small room together with me naked from the waist down, with only a thin sheet over my parts. Parts that he'd seen exactly once, and by seen, I meant had contact with. Because the lights had been off on New Year's Eve, and I sadly—I mean *fortunately*—had no memory of how his body looked naked.

"Your doctor seems to know you well," Chance said from the chair next to the exam table I was on.

"Inside and out," I told him dryly. "Dr. Shah's been my doctor since I was thirteen."

"Did you have problems when you were that young?"

"I always had painful periods, but everyone complains about cramps, so I didn't realize there was anything wrong at first. It kept getting worse though."

"You were Sam's age," he said, frowning. "She doesn't

talk to me about girl things even though I've tried to be open with her, as uncomfortable as that is." He grimaced.

"You'd probably know if there was reason for concern."

I was sitting on the edge of the table, my legs dangling, ankles crossed for some false sense of modesty. I didn't realize I was drumming my fingers on the surface until Chance reached over and covered my hand with his.

"Are you nervous?" he asked.

I was about to deny it until our gazes met and I recognized the concern in his eyes.

"Yes."

"This is routine, right?"

"Yes."

Seconds ticked by in silence. He kept his hand on mine, leaning over from the chair against the wall. Eventually I said, "Being high risk, I'm worried about what they'll find."

"Like?"

"Like no baby forming in the sac. Or no sac. Or anything else abnormal. Which I know sounds odd since none of this was planned, but..."

He scooted his chair closer, then wove our fingers together. I appreciated that touch of concrete support so much.

"Let's think positively," he finally said.

I studied him from my higher perch. "Do you mean that?"

"Why wouldn't I?"

"I mean, you've said you're in this, but I just wondered if... Things would be simpler for you if..."

He squeezed my hand. "Stop. I don't want anything bad to happen. I understand how much you want to be a mom."

I nodded but couldn't think what to say.

"I want you to get what you want, Rowan. And I'm

willing to be at your side for it. So...positive thoughts. Everything is going to be okay."

We'd soon find out, because the door opened, and the ultrasound tech entered.

"Good afternoon. My name is Janie, and I'll be doing your ultrasound today."

We made small talk while she readied the equipment. By now I was so nervous I commented on autopilot. I couldn't have told you what we discussed.

Janie glanced at me and paused her preparations. "Breathe, Rowan. This won't hurt."

I nodded. That wasn't what I was afraid of.

Chance seemed to understand, and he enclosed my hand in his again, standing against the side of the exam table. I was relieved to have him with me, physically close, emotionally supportive. As determined as I was to *not* depend on him, I recognized how reassuring it was to not be alone in this.

"Okay," Janie finally said. "Let's have a look."

I made eye contact with Chance. A connection came alive between us, nearly tangible. In his eyes were empathy and support. For an instant, it was just the two of us in this monumental, private moment. He squeezed my hand and smiled before the moment ended.

I held my breath as the tech got the wand in place, squeezing my eyes shut as I tried not to think about Chance being right there for *that*.

My heart was racing. My bladder was so full I was afraid I was going to embarrass myself, but that thought disappeared the second the screen filled with unidentifiable black and white blobs. I knew enough to understand I wouldn't be able to recognize a tiny human-shaped fetus yet, but that didn't prevent me from tensing up as I waited for the tech to give some indication of what we were looking at.

"What can you tell us?" Chance asked, speaking my thoughts aloud.

The tech was quiet for a few seconds as the images shifted. I held my breath and squeezed the hell out of Chance's hand.

"There's the fetus," the tech said, and I exhaled audibly even though I couldn't tell exactly what we were seeing. She pointed to a tiny blob on the screen. "Everything looks intact so far. I'm going to measure it to see how we're doing for growth."

I kept my eyes locked on the screen even though I couldn't tell much about what she was doing. I couldn't help noticing Chance's gentle fingers brushing my hair away from my face. I wasn't sure he realized he did it, but it calmed me.

A short knock sounded on the door. Then it opened a crack, and Dr. Shah poked her head in. She seemed to study the screen across the room for a couple seconds, then smiled. Somehow that smile reassured me even more.

"Do you mind if I come see?" she asked.

"The more the merrier," Janie said. "Measurements are exactly where they should be."

"Look at your little bean growing in there," Dr. Shah said as she came up to Chance's side.

For the next couple of minutes, Janie pointed out parts of the fetus—little buds that would become limbs, the head, the black areas in it that would become the brain.

I kept my emotions under lock and key, waiting, breathing shallowly, just in case. I was afraid to jump to any happy conclusions prematurely. Maybe they could still spot a problem?

"There's that tiny heart," Dr. Shah said with awe in her voice.

I studied the screen, unsure where to look until Janie pointed out an area where the white seemed to pulse.

My mouth fell open as I tried to comprehend how that minuscule little pulsing would become a full-fledged human heart. The entire fetus was the size of a blueberry, but that little speck was beating away right before our eyes.

My eyes were brimming with tears, I realized. I could barely comprehend this moment and how significant it was.

Before I was ready, the screen went dark, and the viewing session ended.

"Everything looks good, Rowan," Dr. Shah said, her eyes sparkling, giving me confidence. "The body is a wondrous thing."

"Thanks for coming in," I said, knowing that wasn't the norm. She and I had been through a lot together. She'd known me for more than half my life.

"I wouldn't miss it." She glanced at Chance, who we'd told her was the father without explaining our relationship, or lack of one. "I'm really happy for you two. Breathe easy, rest a lot, and give yourself a break whenever you need it."

I nodded and thanked her again.

When I was alone, I quickly got dressed, then opened the door. Chance had waited outside, and he stepped into the room and enfolded me in his arms before I knew what was happening.

I wound my arms around him, closed my eyes, breathed him in. Soaked in the moment, the comfort, the sense that we were in this together. Partners in the most incredible, unimaginable journey.

My friends were supportive, but there was nobody else on this road with us in exactly the same way. We'd created a child together, and the two of us alone were responsible for...everything.

"Thank you," I said into his strong, comforting chest.

He let out a quiet chuckle. "For what? I didn't do anything."

"For being here."

He kissed the top of my head, his arms still around me. "Of course, Rowan."

For how haphazardly we'd found each other on New Year's Eve, he was turning out to be a caring, kind man. I felt incredibly lucky because I knew, from personal experience and from listening to the single teachers I used to work with, the planet was crawling with assholes and jerks.

Chloe's words to describe Chance echoed through my head. *Solid. Not hard to look at.* Beyond that, I knew he was a loving father, even if he and Sam were somewhat disconnected currently. He was generous, unselfish, and smart as hell at his job as well.

Was I attracted to him? Hell to the yes. Even now, as we held on to each other, my blood hummed with desire.

But there was so much more to him than just his body and his pheromones.

I'd sworn off any type of involvement with him because, yes, I was grieving and an emotional mess, but maybe that was premature. I'd be dumb to not give things a chance to develop just because I was vulnerable. As long as I continued to be cautious, as long as I didn't try to force anything, I needed—and our child deserved for me—to keep an open mind about Chance Cordova.

Who knew what the future held for us? Maybe he was the right guy.

It wasn't until we were walking out of the medical building that I noticed Chance had become quiet and tense.

Chapter Nineteen

Chance

Rowan and I didn't speak on our way to her car after the ultrasound.

In truth, I was lost in my head, so it was handy she'd insisted on being the one to drive us into Nashville.

Once we were in the car, she started the engine, then said, "So I have a tradition. Are you in a hurry?"

"No." It was early afternoon. We hadn't had lunch yet, and I wasn't sure how much I'd be able to get my head into work once we returned to the office anyway.

"Are you okay, Chance?" she asked, studying me across the front seat.

I forced a smile and nodded. "Hungry actually."

Her pretty eyes lit up. "I've got you."

She pulled out of the parking garage and drove a couple of miles. When she turned onto Hale Street, my brows went up. Holden, Kemp, and I had been here several times to meet with Hunter Clayborne, the owner of Clayborne's on the Corner, to talk beer. Before taking over his family's bar, he'd been a brand manager for a brewery in Chicago. The dude knew his shit and was generous with his knowledge.

My eyes were on Hunter's bar and grill as Rowan parallel parked on the opposite side of the street.

"Lunch?" I asked.

"Cupcakes."

I realized we were parked directly in front of Sugar Babies Bakery, which was owned by Hunter's wife, Kennedy, and two other women.

"Cupcakes aren't lunch," I said.

"They're my tradition. I started coming here after each appointment when they opened a few years ago. My reward for the trauma of having my insides messed with in various torturous ways."

I couldn't fault that system. I'd been caught off guard when the ultrasound tech had wielded that wand. I didn't remember Erin having anything so invasive with Sam.

Not only was I too hungry for just cupcakes, but Rowan needed all the nutrients and protein she could get. Last I knew, cupcakes weren't good for that. "You're nurturing a blueberry-size being in there. We can have cupcakes *after* we eat real food."

She bit her lip and hesitated as if she'd actually thought a cupcake lunch was okay. "You're mean."

"Come on, Mama," I said. "Time to be the grown-up."

She stuck her tongue out at me. "Where do you want to go?"

I pointed at Clayborne's. "Have you been there before?"

She shook her head.

"Great burgers. Big menu. And I know the owner."

As we crossed the street, I told her how Hunter had helped us with branding when Rusty Anchor had first opened. "Maybe you know his wife, Kennedy? She handles Henry's marketing and is part owner of Sugar Babies."

"I don't, but if she's responsible for that"—she gestured over her shoulder at the bakery—"she's already my hero."

We walked in the main door of Clayborne's. Several tables were occupied, but there were open ones since it was well after the usual lunch hour. I led her to a high-top table tucked into a corner by the stairs.

Within two minutes, Hunter himself showed up at our table. "Hey, Chance. It's good to see you." He extended a hand, and I shook it.

"You too. This is Rowan Andrews. She works at the Anchor with me. Turns out she's a fan of your wife's bakery."

Hunter smiled warmly as he and Rowan shook hands. "I am too. One of the many ways Kennedy won me over was by bringing me cupcakes."

"I haven't met her, but she seems pretty brilliant to me," Rowan said.

"She is."

"You waiting tables now?" I asked him.

He laughed. "Some days, but not today. Becca will be over in a minute to get your drink orders. I just stopped by to say hi. Thanks for coming in."

"You bet," I said before he headed up the stairs to his office.

Rowan and I ordered and made small talk, managing to completely ignore the life-changing appointment we'd just come from. I was grateful for shallow topics.

Once our burgers arrived, Rowan brought an end to the easiness by asking, "Chance, what's going through your head?"

My brows shot up. "I'm hungry." That wasn't a lie. It was going on two p.m. Breakfast was a long time ago.

She took a bite, but I could tell she wasn't appeased by my answer as she watched me thoughtfully.

"You've been tense since we left the clinic. Are you having second thoughts?"

I shook my head as I shoved my burger in my mouth. She continued to watch me, which told me I wasn't going to get away with changing the subject. Didn't mean I had to offer her more info.

"You were right. This burger is delicious," she said. "And the pretzel bites... I might need to expand my tradition to pretzel bites with cheese sauce, *then* cupcakes."

"What's your favorite cupcake?" Maybe she'd forget to go back to questioning me.

"Last time I was in, they had a chocolate bourbon pecan pie that was memorable. Or there's toasted s'mores, Oreo, turtle, butterscotch crunch... I can't pick a favorite."

"Do they have vanilla?" I asked dryly.

She stopped chewing and stared at me as if I'd grown a second head. After swallowing her food, she said, "I imagine so on some days. Is that what you're going to get?"

I chuckled. "I don't know. I'll have to see what my choices are."

"Their baker is creative. She dreams up amazing flavors. If you've changed your mind about the baby, you need to let me know, Chance."

I took a drink to wash down the food that got stuck in my throat. Shaking my head, I said, "I haven't changed my mind. I'm here for you, and I'll be here for the baby." The words came out with extra force and more emotion than I'd intended. Enough that Rowan tilted her head and studied me as she chewed her food.

"I come from a family that wasn't supportive," I said, delving into a topic I didn't like discussing. "My dad is the head of surgery, and my mom is a neurosurgeon at the same hospital in St. Louis."

Rowan's brows shot up. "I've wondered about your family. Wondered if our baby would have a big one on your side, because it's just me on this side."

I shook my head. "Just my parents and my older brother, Devin. He's a cardiologist, by the way."

"Wow. You have a very medical family. Did you consider going into medicine?"

"Not once. I saw the downside from a front-row seat."

"What's the downside?"

"My parents' careers completely dominate their lives. My brother and I were raised by nannies and babysitters while they both worked eighty-hour weeks. That's not the kind of life I want, not for myself or for my kid. Kids," I corrected.

Rowan frowned. "That sounds...extreme. And awful for you."

I shrugged. "There were two or three good nannies in there, but yeah. Extreme is one word for it. Self-important is another. My dad has a god complex. Both of them do. They don't *have* to work that much; they choose to. They're a perfect match and at the top of their fields, but they never should've had kids."

"Are you close to your brother?"

"Nope. He went their route. Workaholic, thinks the world can't turn without him doing his thing. I haven't talked to him in probably three years."

"I'm sorry, Chance. That sounds like a tough childhood."

I shook my head, let out a sardonic laugh. "Don't feel

sorry for me. I had everything a kid could want. All my needs were covered."

"Except their time and affection," she guessed, hitting the nail on the head.

"I've always sworn I'd be the opposite of them. My kid comes first. Only problem is my kid doesn't want anything to do with me."

"That's not true."

"I don't need her to want to hang out with me. I just feel perpetually helpless as a father. And then seeing that beating heart on the monitor today..." I shook my head, overcome as I remembered that moment. "When you first told me you were pregnant, it took a little while for it to sink in, but it did. Or I thought it did. Today was...more real. Like 3D real. Like how can I be a father of two when I'm fucking up royally with one?"

"You're not fucking up."

"It sure feels like it when my daughter hides in the basement and barely says two words during dinner."

"She's a teenager," she said as if that was the end-all, be-all explanation for everything.

"That's a copout."

"I worked with teenagers for three years. They're moody, self-centered, and everything causes angst. From what I've seen, Sam's a good kid at the heart of everything."

"She is. She's so damn smart, Rowan. She's always gotten straight A's, but now that she's in high school, when it really starts to matter..." I shook my head.

Rowan seemed to be thinking that over. "Adolescence is hard," she said. "Especially for girls. Especially without a mom."

"I've always tried to be both dad and mom to her."

"I bet you've done an amazing job of it."

I scoffed.

"You said it yourself. Certain topics are harder for a dad with a teenage girl. Have you ever grown boobs? Bled for several days a month?"

I cringed. "So, what, I shouldn't even try?"

"You should always try. That doesn't mean she'll accept it." She took a drink of her decaf coffee, set down her mug. "I was super close to my grandpa when I was little." Her gaze went distant, and a smile crept over her lips. "He used to play 'school' with me." She laughed. "He always let me be the teacher."

The image of a pint-sized Rowan with a whiteboard made me smile.

"He played basketball with me too. Taught me some fundamentals. We played so many games of Horse. When puberty started though? I went to Gram for everything. I still loved Gramps dearly, but our relationship changed."

"You and Sam bonded more in your first five minutes in our house than she and I have for months," I said, beginning to understand her point.

"I can see that. Because fashion. Most boys don't generally get it."

"I can't argue with that."

"My situation wasn't like everyone else's, but I know from my friends, mother-daughter relationships are unlike anything else. Moms drive their daughters nuts, but also daughters sometimes just need their moms. Or a mother figure. Gram was that for me. Someone to tell them no matter how exciting it is to get your first bra, it sucks to wear one for the rest of your life. Someone to assure them the heartache caused by an unrequited crush will pass."

I realized I didn't really know whether Sam was interested in boys yet. The little shit at the beach was the first one I'd heard about other than a crush a few months back, which I'd effectively discouraged. Did she have a crush on the beach jackass? Someone else? I didn't ever ask anymore, because I knew I'd want to run him out of town if she did, whoever it was.

A mom would be different, I guessed.

"Maybe you could spend time with Sam..." I let my words trail off and shook my head, instantly regretting what I'd said.

"I'd love to get to know your daughter."

"Getting to know her is fine, but I can't ask you to do more than that. I can't really even ask you to get to know her."

"Sure you can. You've gone out of your way for me by giving me an affordable place to live."

"I told you that wasn't selfless."

"Hanging out with Sam wouldn't be selfless either. I happen to like teenagers. Connecting with one is one of the most rewarding feelings in the world for a teacher."

"This isn't a teacher-student relationship we're talking about here."

"No, and it's not mother-daughter either. Maybe friendship. Maybe a female confidante. Maybe just another pesky adult in her space. Who knows how she'll react? I'm not her mom, and I would never try to be, but I'd be happy to spend time with her if she'll go for it."

It was my turn to study her face, to see if I could discern any doubts or hesitation.

"You'd really be okay with that?"

She smiled genuinely. "Whatever Sam will go for, I'm up for it."

I blew out a big breath. "I don't know how to thank you for that."

"Kind of like I don't know how to thank you for letting me live almost rent-free. Let's just call it even. You're helping me. I'm helping you—potentially, if Sam will give it a chance."

"If Sam will give it a chance, I'll owe you everything."

"You'll owe me nothing, Chance. Even stephen. No arguing."

I looked one more time for any sign of trepidation on her face, but there was none. "Okay. Thank you."

As we finished our meal, we both became silent, lost in our thoughts. On the one hand, I was grateful and relieved she was taking an interest in my daughter. Maybe a female role model or friend was what Sam needed.

On the other hand, I couldn't help thinking that, if Sam was receptive, this would intertwine our lives even more deeply, and that made me nervous as hell.

Chapter Twenty

Rowan

I'd lived with Chance for two weeks now.

My feelings for him were deepening every day, even if I tried not to acknowledge them. We ate dinner together each evening and, more times than not, hung out in the family room afterwards, whether we had the TV on or got carried away with a conversation or even just sat quietly reading our own things.

Spending time with him was more than just comfortable. I found myself looking forward to our evenings together. Even if they did result in wild dreams starring him as more than just a friend or roommate.

I was slowly getting to know his daughter better too. I got the sense she longed for the female companionship, and I thrived on our connection too.

Maybe it was dumb or overstepping, but I'd picked up a Valentine's gift for Sam.

It was after eleven p.m. when I spotted the hair clips and box of candy I'd spontaneously grabbed at the Country

Market, sitting on the dresser in my room. Tomorrow was V Day, and I wanted her to start her day with a present. I remembered all too well how it felt to go through February fourteenth with no boyfriend and no valentines.

Chance drove Sam to school each morning, and they usually left before I made it downstairs, so I picked up the items plus a cute card and gift bag for the clips and crept out of my room in my leggings and a long-sleeve pajama tee. Chance's bedroom door was closed, and I suspected he was watching TV from the faint light under the door. He'd admitted he often fell asleep with it on, just like I had so many nights in my Gram's last months.

The rest of the house was dark, so I lit the way with my phone.

It'd been a week since my ultrasound and my promise to Chance to get to know his daughter. The promise wasn't necessary, as I had every intention of it anyway. From our first meeting, Sam hadn't been what I'd expected from Chance's few comments about her.

She seemed like a sweet girl who was struggling to find her place in this world. She had a pretty smile that didn't quite erase the hint of sadness from her eyes.

My pregnancy sugar cravings were real, and yesterday I'd convinced Sam to help me make chocolate peanut butter cupcakes. Neither one of us had much prior cupcake experience, but the dazzling selection at Sugar Babies last week had inspired me. Inspired me and had me daydreaming about all the flavors I'd passed up to settle for a single chocolate peppermint.

The bakery here in town, Sugar, specialized in cookies and donuts. I'd indulged in my share of those, but nothing swayed my need for a rich, fluffy cupcake with a big mound of sweet, creamy frosting.

Our baking endeavor had been one of the first times Sam and I had spent more than a few random minutes together outside of dinners. At first she'd been shy, but the more we chatted, the more she'd opened up. I hadn't pried, but with Chance occupied by a hockey game in the other room, she'd confessed she didn't have any friends except a girl named Kinsley, who was in several of her classes.

From what I gathered, Kinsley was brainy and not popular, which Sam made sound like a strike against her. In my eyes, it was the perfect opportunity to deepen the friendship. I'd mildly suggested that, being careful not to come across as parental or teacher-ish. Sometimes a girl just needed some low-key girl talk.

Our cupcakes turned out ugly and homemade-looking compared to the works of art at Sugar Babies, but they tasted sublime.

In the kitchen now, I turned on the dim light over the stove and located a pen so I could sign the humorous Valentine card. As I was stuffing the card in the envelope, Chance came down the stairs.

"Hey, what are you doing down here?" he asked in a hushed voice as he entered the kitchen.

Holy hell. Apparently I was feeding my fantasies with some man fodder.

He wore gray sweatpants and a black tee that stretched across his chest. His feet were bare, hair sexily mussed, and his biceps bulged appealingly where his sleeves ended.

I swallowed and tore my gaze away to the candy. "I picked up a Valentine gift for Sam. I'm setting it out so she sees it in the morning. It's not much, just a little something so she doesn't have a sucky Valentine's Day, in case she doesn't get anything else."

"From what I've heard, she won't get anything else," he

said sadly. "And I am a shithead of a father. I didn't even think about giving her something."

I held the box of candy out to him.

"She'll love that," he said.

"You can give it to her. I'll give her the hair clips." I held up the three pack of flower-shaped clips similar to the one she'd complimented when I wore it, then placed it in the gift bag. "And the card, because I already wrote in it, and you and I aren't quite on joint gift-giving levels."

"Not quite." He looked from the candy to my face. "I'll owe you big-time."

I shook my head. "Remember we're not keeping score? There's a place on the back for to and from. I didn't write anything yet."

"Thank you. Double thank you. I really bombed that."

"There's no rule that dads have to get their kids a Valentine."

"Doesn't mean it won't make her day better." He scrawled a message on the candy box, and we set the gifts on the counter where Sam couldn't miss them.

"I hope so. I've always told myself it's a pointless Hallmark-hyped holiday, but that only goes so far when the girl next to you gloats about roses and candy."

He nodded. "Surely you had a lot of boyfriends though," he said, his tone teasing.

I didn't have to think long to accurately say, "I've never had a guy get me anything for Valentine's Day."

His smile dropped. "Never?"

I shook my head. "I've only had one relationship that lasted longer than a few months, and he turned out to be not a gem."

"In high school?"

I laughed. "Ever."

He pegged me with a skeptical look.

"Fact," I said.

He crossed the kitchen to the cupcake container, opened it, and took one out. "This is what I came down for. Want one?"

"Of course." As if I could turn down an ugly cupcake. I walked over to that corner of the kitchen and took one.

"Tell me about the not-a-gem guy. When was that?" Chance leaned against the stove as he unwrapped his cake.

I settled against the cabinets that were at a right angle to him, swiped a finger through the peanut-butter cream frosting, and stuck it in my mouth, closing my eyes in appreciation. "I met Christian when I was still teaching. He tended bar at a place my teacher friends and I used to go for happy hour."

"How long were you together?"

"About a year and a half." The sweet cupcake was doing its best to counteract the unpleasantness of the topic.

"So he definitely had an opportunity to do Valentine's Day right."

I laughed dryly. "He had an opportunity to do a lot of things right."

"But he was not a gem," Chance said between bites.

"We'd been together a few months when I moved in with my grandmother. She'd started confusing her daily pills, her meals...a lot of things. She hid how much she was struggling from me, but there came a point when she couldn't hide it anymore. My lease ended, and it was an easy decision for me. Christian didn't like it. He thought I should move in with him."

"And do what with your grandmother?" he asked, disbelief in his tone.

I just shook my head because that seemed rhetorical.

"At that point, I was still working. I couldn't go out as much because Gram sundowned pretty badly—evenings were her most confused and agitated time." I said all of this without letting my mind go too deep into memories. "I invited him over instead, for dinner, a movie, whatever, thinking it was a decent compromise."

"He didn't agree?"

"He put up with it for a few weeks before he started complaining. By the time I quit my job, it was pretty clear we weren't going to last. To be fair, I didn't have much time or energy for anything besides Gram. I can't really blame him for ending our relationship."

"But Valentine's Day is different. We *can* blame him for that," Chance said lightly, then stuck the last of his cupcake into his mouth.

I appreciated that lightness so much.

"For sure we can blame him for that. So which kind of boyfriend were you? Did you nail V Day or screw it up?" I asked.

"Growing up, I usually nailed it." He went thoughtful while he rolled up his empty cupcake paper. "Even when I was married, I always did something for Valentine's. The last few years, I don't think it mattered," he said gravely. "But I still kept trying."

There was something heavy in his tone, his words, besides sadness or grief. I tried to put my finger on what, but he avoided my gaze.

"You said she was an addict," I said carefully, wanting to know more if he would go there. Wanting to acknowledge this part of his history if he would. If we were going to co-parent for two decades, it seemed important to know him better.

"Flowers and candy couldn't measure up to a pill," he

said quietly. "*I* couldn't measure up to a pill." His voice was raw.

I reached over and squeezed his arm, unable to *not* touch him, to try to assuage some of his pain. "Chance…"

He shook his head, like he was trying to shake it off. "I'm okay. Just…having someone choose drugs over you… It messes with a person."

My heart cracked for him, for the pain he still carried. Not just grief and loss—God knew those alone were horrible—but Chance had extra scars.

"I think addiction can take the choice away from people," I said. "It was never a fair battle between you and drugs."

"Yeah," he said on an emotion-laden exhalation. "Sorry that came out." He tried to smile, as if we could blow off that heavy moment, but it was just a flicker of a grin. "Being married to an addict does lifelong things to a guy's head."

Without giving myself a chance to waver, I closed the space between us and put my arms around him, hurting for him, wishing there was some way to help him hurt less. A few heartbeats passed before I felt his hands on my back, wrapping around me, pulling me closer.

He smelled like strength and comfort, even though I was the one trying to comfort him. I breathed him in, trying to figure out what else I could say.

Before I could settle on anything, he pulled his head up, loosened his grasp, and nudged my chin up so our eyes met. Without warning, he lowered his lips to mine and kissed me, not like a friend who appreciated comfort or a late-night chat but like a man who'd been aching to kiss me for days.

In half a second, my body reacted, an ache awakening deep in my core as his tongue plundered my mouth aggressively. I kissed him back with no hesitation, no thought, just instinct and need. I ran my fingers through his coarse hair, pressing myself into him, reveling in the feel of his erection against me, confirmation that our attraction was still two-sided and very much alive.

He slid his hands down my back, slipped them under my shirt, and caressed my bare skin as we devoured each other's mouth.

Quick, heavy footsteps sounded on the basement stairs. Chance reacted before I did, ending the kiss abruptly, whipping his hands from under my shirt, standing straighter. Just before the basement door creaked open, I stepped away from him, putting space between us and leaning against the counter, hoping like hell I looked calm and casual instead of flushed and turned on.

"Sam," Chance said as she took the last step up to the kitchen. "What are you doing up?"

His daughter pressed a hand to her chest as her gaze bounced between us. "You scared me."

"Sorry about that. You should be in bed, shouldn't you?" he said.

"History test tomorrow. I'm studying. Need a snack." She narrowed her eyes and looked from him to me and back again. "What's going on here?"

"Nothing," Chance said.

Terrible, guilty-sounding answer.

"Cupcake run," I said, grabbing the container from the counter and holding it out to her, hoping sugar would distract her from her flustered father.

She glanced at the container and shook her head. "I'm in salt mode." As she headed toward the pantry, she eyed us suspiciously again. "So you're both just hanging out in the kitchen, having a midnight snack?"

"I was lying there thinking about the cupcakes,"

Chance said, finally seeming to snap into nonguilty mode. "Rowan was here when I came down."

She hadn't noticed the Valentine gifts yet. I debated using them as a distraction now. It would ruin the surprise for the morning but offer an explanation for why we were in the kitchen.

"How much studying do you have left?" Chance asked.

I put the cupcakes back in their corner on the counter, then washed my hands, striving for nonchalance and normalcy. *Just finishing up my midnight snack. Not kissing your dad at all.*

"Oh, just a review of the Civil War," she answered.

My brows shot up.

"Is that all?" Chance asked dryly.

"A review, Dad. I've read the chapters."

"Need someone to quiz you?" I offered as I turned around from the sink.

Sam seemed to consider it briefly, then said, "I'm almost done, but thanks for offering."

"If you ever want help, especially with science"—I raised my hand—"I'm your girl. I miss teaching."

"Biology is my favorite class," Sam said.

Chance looked surprised.

"What?" Sam asked. "You know I like science the best."

"It's just that you haven't talked much about your classes. I'm glad to hear you like biology. Cells and mitochondria and DNA, right? Good stuff."

Sam grinned. "You've told me before you didn't like any science classes."

Chance flicked a nervous glance my way, and I laughed.

"Really?" I asked.

"I was better at writing and reading," he said, shrugging. "I'm a word guy."

"Just a word guy living with two STEM girls," I said, smiling at Sam.

"This is my lot in life," he joked. "I'm just happy my daughter's studying."

"It's not like I have a social life," Sam said matter-of-factly. She pulled a bag of tortilla chips out, then took the hummus container from the fridge. "Might as well get back to it so I can sleep."

"Sleep sounds good. Gonna try that myself." Chance kissed the top of Sam's head quickly, then headed out of the kitchen. "Night, STEM girls."

"Night," we said at the same time.

"Good luck," I told Sam.

"Thanks. Night, Rowan," she said, then carried her snacks to the stairs, closed the door, and thundered back down, not noticing her presents.

Then I was back where I started, alone in the kitchen. Except this time, my insides were still cooling down from Chance's kisses.

I couldn't help noticing how fast he'd run off, even before his daughter had gone back downstairs. It was as if he didn't want to be caught alone with me again.

Chapter Twenty-One

Chance

Nearly twenty-four hours later, Rowan and I hadn't had a private moment since I'd kissed her last night, and I was good with that. I wouldn't know what to say other than *whoops, I fucked up*. Something told me that wouldn't land right.

The fact was, at the time, it hadn't felt like a fuckup. It'd felt...

Dammit. Stop thinking about it.

Today had been utter chaos at work, but that was to be expected when we had a large event at the brewery.

Tonight was Rusty Anchor's Ode to Love and Beer event —a Valentine's celebration that highlighted our two seasonal beers. Henry's was catering it with heavy appetizers and finger foods, many of which would complement the chocolate stout and the cherry wheat. We'd hired Adrian Cormier to DJ later on, with the lower level open for dancing.

Our marketing had targeted not only couples but friend

groups, and tickets had sold out. In addition, we'd invited six parties who'd inquired about using the brewery for their upcoming events. We hoped to convince them to book our venue by letting them experience it in action.

I'd brought my party clothes to work with me, knowing from experience I'd likely not have time to go home and change beforehand. No matter how much preparation we did in advance, shit always came up last minute. Tonight that was in the form of an incorrect QR code on the posters that advertised the brewery as a rental venue. Somewhere we'd gotten our QRs crossed, and they linked to the wrong page.

I'd happened to test one of the codes out a half hour before go time, just a routine check. That had given me just enough time to go back to my office, print out the correct codes, then affix them over the incorrect ones.

Guests were beginning to arrive as I'd rehung the posters in their inconspicuous spots. I'd rushed off to get myself ready. Now I was in the private restroom in Holden's office, changing into my navy chinos, dark gray jacket, and a light gray sweater underneath.

When I emerged, Holden walked into his office. "Hey, there you are," he said. "Looking sharp, my friend."

"Thanks. Posters are fixed. Everything else okay?"

He went to his desk chair and grabbed the jacket he'd shed earlier, which told me prep time was officially over. "As far as I know." He pulled on the jacket, glanced at the open door, and lowered his voice. "Hey, Chloe told me about you and Rowan." His brows climbed up his forehead as if asking for verification. "I've been trying to find a private moment all day to bring it up."

Rowan had told me she'd let Chloe in on our secret a

few days ago, so I wasn't surprised, just a little taken off guard by him bringing it up right now.

"Did she tell you all of it?" I asked as he reached my side, still adjusting his jacket.

"The baby? Or is there more?"

With a chuckle, I said, "That isn't enough?"

"That's a lot. And she's living with you?"

"She couldn't find a place."

"Yeah, I've heard that's tough right now. Are you two...?"

"No. We're"—I looked away—"roommates. Getting to know each other as friends." Kissing her popped into my mind, and I shoved it down.

"Maybe more?" Holden asked. "She's easy to like."

I shook my head. "Not more. With Sam and now another one on the way, I've got more than I can handle, and so does she. We're both good with keeping it platonic."

He watched me a couple of seconds longer than necessary, as if he didn't believe me.

"Really," I said. "The stakes are high. Neither of us wants to risk getting further involved and having it not work out. Not when we have eighteen years of co-parenting ahead of us."

He nodded once. "That's understandable, I guess, if there's no chemistry."

Oh, there was fucking chemistry. Judging by last night, the chemistry was highly flammable. But that didn't mean we had to give in to it. I'd managed to not give in to it every night except last night so far. Last night I'd made a mistake, but it wouldn't happen again.

"She plans to move out once she's back on her feet," I assured him. "Shall we get the hell to our own party?"

"That's a plan. I hope to find time to eat. The food smells incredible."

We headed out of his office together, down the short hall, and entered the public room on the main level.

Dozens of guests milled around, some couples, some larger groups as we'd hoped, all of them dressed to the hilt, and most of them with a beer in their hand. The noise level was loud and festive.

"My sister-in-law looks like she's about to pop," Holden said.

I followed his gaze to Ava and Cash. Ava, who was only a handful of weeks out from her due date, wore a hot pink thigh-length dress that gathered above her very pregnant belly then draped over her baby bump. On her feet were matching hot-pink glittery sneakers. Cash hovered over her as if he was afraid she might go into labor in the next five minutes.

Holden headed for them, but I stayed back, scanning the room for any of our six special-guest parties who were in the market for a venue. I wasn't going to hard-sell them, but I would give them a little special treatment.

I didn't spot any of them, so I strode along the windowed side of the room that showed off the brewhouse, still searching, still coming up empty. I'd check again later.

When I turned, I stopped in my tracks at the vision before me.

Rowan had just come in the from the offices. She stood at the other end of the crowd, as I had, giving me the chance to soak up her beauty before she saw me.

She wore a short burgundy dress with off-the-shoulder sleeves and a sequined neckline that dipped low enough to give me and the world a sample of her cleavage. It was by no means risqué, was perfectly appropriate for a work event.

But the images that flashed through my mind were anything but suitable for the office.

I forced my gaze away before she saw me, then headed to the stairs to check on the guests up there. I was going to need some time to cool my thoughts off, plus a whole lot of self-coaching, before I interacted with the knockout mother of my unborn child.

———

Rowan

Two hours into it, the Ode to Love and Beer party was, from my inexperienced perspective, turning out to be a sparkling success.

We'd sold out tickets. Beer was flowing. Merch was selling like crazy. Moods were flying high, and compliments on the seasonal flavors abounded. Everyone raved about the food as well.

Everything was coming up roses and romance for this company I was beginning to genuinely love.

In spite of the joy and success surrounding me, my agitation grew as the night went on.

Though Chance and I had both been at work since eight this morning, often in the same room, working on the same thing, he had yet to say anything personal to me.

That kiss last night had him running scared, and while a part of me was amused, that wasn't going to fly. Not when we lived and worked together. He'd been the one to say we needed to communicate.

The time had come for me to force communication.

I excused myself from the upstairs table of Chloe's friends, who were becoming my friends too—Presley, Anna, and Olivia—and went to the stairs. I'd seen Chance head down a few minutes ago.

The main floor was even more crowded than the upper level, with a huddle of people around the serving counter, another few gathered at the merch station, and the area we'd roped off as the dance floor overflowing.

Holden and Kemp stood near the floor-to-ceiling window to the brewhouse, filling their men-of-the-hour roles jovially as a continuous flow of guests mingled with them. I had no doubt everyone was singing their praises, as they deserved. I'd allowed myself one taste of Kemp's Love Is the Pits, mainly to see what everyone was talking about. It was dangerously delicious.

I eventually spotted Chance talking with a group I realized might be his dad group. A couple of the guys were without dates, and several had brought their wives or fiancées. I'd met Knox, Holden's brother, and his wife, Quincy. I was guessing the other couple was Max, the football coach, and Harper, who owned Earthly Charm on the square.

I kept Chance in my sights as I mingled my way closer, stopping to talk to guests, asking them their opinions of the seasonal brews, and making sure they didn't want for anything. I was biding my time, waiting for the right moment.

That moment came when the first notes of "All of Me" played over the speakers.

I beelined toward my sexy prey, who looked sharp and irresistible tonight—if you weren't irritated with his cowardice over last night.

I sidled up near him as the couples in his group headed off to the dance floor.

"Hey," I said.

"Hey, yourself." He smiled, but I sensed an edge of uneasiness beneath the surface, as if he understood I wasn't here to talk about work.

"Let's go dance," I said.

"Don't you want me to introduce you to West and Luke—"

"I want to dance." I took his hand and tugged him away from his friends, who weren't paying attention to us.

As he followed me toward the dance floor, he said in my ear, "Are you sure this is a good idea?"

I didn't answer until we were in the middle of the dancing couples, my hands on his shoulders, his on my waist. "Sometimes coworkers dance at their company's party. It's fine. No one will think, *oh, I bet she's having his baby*."

He zipped a gaze around us at that, then seemed to understand no one could hear me. It was too loud, and people were wrapped up in their own twosomes.

"Just two coworkers sharing a dance to celebrate," I said. "That's what it looks like."

"Got it. You're right."

Before he could let his guard down, I said, "You've been avoiding me."

"I've been working with you all day long."

I nodded. "But last night, you literally ran off before Sam could leave us alone."

"It was late."

"Chance, stop it. To quote a guy, we need to communicate. Not run scared."

We swayed in silence for a bit, with me letting up so he could think.

"I owe you an apology," he eventually said. "I went against our agreement."

That wasn't the angle I'd expected him to take. "I wasn't upset about that."

"I shouldn't have done it."

We swayed to the slow tempo, our bodies an appropriate coworker distance apart, which required effort to maintain because, in spite of being annoyed with him all day, I wanted to feel his body against mine. I waited, sensing he had more to say.

"Erin's a tough subject," he said. "Kissing you is much more pleasant." His mouth curved into a boyish grin, dimple appearing.

I fought not to be affected by that smile that had the power to melt me. "So it was a diversion tactic?"

He tilted his head in thought. "*Tactic* makes it sound cold and calculated. There was nothing cold about that kiss."

I lost my battle to stay irritated, my own mouth flirting with a grin as I remembered the heat of that kiss. "No, there wasn't."

Our eyes met, and that pull between us was strong.

Another couple brushed against us from the side, popping us out of our connection, bringing us back to the here and now.

"Anyway," Chance said, "Sam nearly walking in on us was a perfect reminder of why that can't happen."

"She was suspicious," I acknowledged. "We need to tell her the truth."

"I know. I'm working up to it. That'll be...humbling." He frowned, and I understood what he meant.

We hadn't done anything wrong. We were two consenting adults. But I could see how a one-night stand might seem like a poor example for his teenage daughter.

"I can be by your side when you tell her if you want me

to. Or you can tell her in private. Whatever you think will go over better."

He nodded once. "I'm not sure yet. Either way, it's not going to go over well."

"No. It needs to be soon though. It's getting hard to button my jeans."

His gaze darted down toward my middle even though we stood too close for him to see anything. There was something so intimate about the secret we shared, the knowledge that my body was changing because of him. Whether we ever kissed again, he'd made it clear we were in this together, through the good, bad, and ugly.

If his daughter found out I was pregnant before we told her, the situation could quickly turn ugly.

Chapter Twenty-Two

Rowan

Nausea hit me before I even opened my eyes the following Wednesday morning.

I lay there taking deep, even breaths, staving it off, wondering if I'd eaten something bad or if this was just today's version of morning sickness. I'd had a couple days of feeling pretty decent upon waking. Maybe my body was catching up after that reprieve.

I reached for the box of oyster crackers I'd started keeping on my nightstand and groaned when I remembered it was empty. I'd forgotten to buy a new box.

Closing my eyes again, I lay back on my pillow and focused on my breathing. The minutes ticked by, meaning I'd have to hurry to get to work on time, but that seemed preferable to standing at the moment.

After several minutes of not moving a muscle other than to breathe, the icky feeling receded, not gone entirely, but enough that I thought I could make it to the shower.

I put my hair up so I wouldn't have to dry and style it,

then stepped under the hot water. As I soaped myself, I started to feel better still.

"I might make it through the day yet," I said aloud as I dried off, still moving slowly, afraid of unsettling my gut again.

By the time I was dressed, the house was silent. Chance and Sam would've left a few minutes ago to get her to school on time.

After one more slow, settling breath, I grabbed my purse and bag and headed downstairs. I was halfway down the steps when the bacon smell hit me.

Normally I loved bacon, but today that smell... A tidal wave of nausea rolled through my gut.

I just needed to grab a couple of protein bars from the cabinet, stuff them in my bag, and get out of the house, away from the odor.

I breathed through my mouth, exaggerated and audible, as I hurried to the kitchen cabinet. Before I could get the bars out of the box, I dropped my bags and dashed to the bathroom.

As I was leaning over the toilet emptying my stomach, the door to the garage slammed shut.

"Rowan? Oh, my God, are you okay?" Sam asked from the doorway of the powder room.

With my elbow braced on the cold porcelain, my hand supporting my forehead, I attempted a yes, but even I could hear it wasn't convincing. I retched again, mortified to have an audience but unable to stop it.

My eyes filled with tears, and I felt like an alien had taken control of my body.

Behind me, I heard Sam gagging as she backed away from the doorway.

"Sorry, Rowan," she called. A few seconds later, as I

wiped my mouth with a piece of toilet paper, Sam's voice was back in the doorway but muffled, like she'd pulled her shirt over her face. "Do you want me to get my dad?"

I shook my head, sitting up straighter, testing myself. I felt marginally better now that I'd apparently purged everything in my gut. "No," I managed. "I'm fine."

"That didn't seem fine."

Grabbing the pedestal sink, I pulled myself up and stood, leaned over the basin, and splashed cold water on my face. When I straightened, I saw Sam take a couple steps back from the doorway. I met her gaze in the mirror.

"Sorry," she said. "I don't want to catch whatever you have."

"It's not contagious." I said it without thinking, then pumped soap into my hands and scrubbed them.

"Did you eat something bad?" she asked. "We all had the same beef stir-fry last night, but I feel okay."

"It's not from food," I said, gauging how I felt now. Better still. I could probably handle work as long as I didn't start feeling worse again.

"Oh, my God," Sam said. "Are you pregnant? Is this morning sickness?"

I dried my hands and face, thinking I should replace the towel, when her questions hit me.

Shit.

Again I made eye contact through the mirror, my mind spinning through options. I could lie, or I could tell her the truth before Chance was ready. I didn't like to lie, and it would be the stupidest lie anyway, as reality would prove otherwise within weeks.

"I am," I finally said.

I no sooner got the words out than the door to the garage shut again.

"What's going on?" Chance asked his daughter. He couldn't see into the bathroom from the utility room.

Sam looked to me, which had Chance peeking into the bathroom.

"Rowan was hurling," she said.

"Damn." Chance stepped closer. "Morning sickness?" he asked me.

I nodded, wiping my face with the towel one more time.

He put a hand on my back. "Is there anything I can do to help?"

"You knew she was pregnant," Sam stated instead of questioned.

"Do you want some tea or water?" Chance asked me, not seeming to hear Sam.

"Not yet," I said. "The bacon smell just hit me wrong."

"Oh, my God, is the baby yours, Dad?"

I snapped my gaze to Chance's. My panic was reflected in his eyes.

"Dad?"

My heart hammered while Sam looked from her dad to me and back, her eyes narrowed. This was Chance's question to answer. I held my breath, waiting to hear what he would say.

"Why don't we move out of the bathroom?" Chance said.

Sam held on to the doorjamb, blocking our way.

"It's a simple yes-no question." Sam's tone was harder. "Rowan? Is he the father?"

"Yes," Chance snapped. Then he closed his eyes and seemed to gather his patience. "This wasn't how I planned to tell you, Sam. Can we please sit down?" He gestured to the kitchen.

Sam stepped back, looking as if someone had slapped her.

Chance put his hand on her shoulder, and she jerked away.

I'd never been so torn in my life. I wanted to hug Sam and assure her everything would be okay. I ached to comfort Chance and remind him this was the reaction we'd expected and that she'd come around. And there was a big part of me that itched to grab my bag, run away from the turmoil and bacon odor, and bury my head.

"Let's sit in the family room," Chance said.

"I have school," Sam said, her tone conveying she'd prefer to escape as well.

"Okay. I'll drive you there in five minutes and call in for you so they don't mark you late. This is *not* how I wanted to do this, but I obviously can't control a damn thing." He stepped into the kitchen and turned on the exhaust fan above the stove. "Maybe that'll help," he said to me.

That simple, thoughtful gesture put me on the verge of tears. I fought to hide them. The last thing Sam needed to witness right now was me turning into an emotional mess. "Thanks," I managed as I leaned against the wall, more in the hall than the kitchen.

"I don't want to miss English," Sam snapped impatiently.

Chance leaned against the cabinets, crossing his arms, looking weary. "Rowan is pregnant. Yes, I'm the father. We didn't plan this, obviously."

"God, how embarrassing," Sam muttered. "So you moved your girlfriend in and lied to me? Pretended she's a coworker?"

"I do work at the brewery," I said, feeling helpless, knowing this conversation was ultimately Chance's domain but still wanting to soothe both of them. "And I'm not your dad's girlfriend."

"Better yet," Sam said with an exaggerated laugh, her gaze aimed at Chance. "So you had a one-night stand, got a girl pregnant, and moved her in?"

My brows shot up, because yeah, that was pretty much spot on, and it didn't sound great, particularly from Sam's perspective.

Chance's jaw was clenched tight, his eyes closed. I had to fight not to reach out to him.

"Rowan and I are adults. We've done nothing wrong. We took a risk, and now we're handling the consequences."

"Are you getting married?" Sam asked.

"No. We're planning to co-parent," Chance said.

"So Rowan's living here permanently?"

"Only until I can get my feet under me and find a place of my own," I said. "I'm sorry our actions are affecting you, Sam. Your dad's first concern all along has been you and your feelings."

Sam scoffed. "Obviously not if he was out having a one-night stand."

"Like I said, we're adults, Sam. Rowan and I have a lot to figure out," Chance said. "I'm sorry you found out the way you did."

"I need to get to school." She hurried past me, out of the house.

I spotted a textbook on the counter. "Does she need this?"

"That's why we came back." Chance took it from me. "I'm sorry your morning is shit, Rowan."

The understatement of that made my lips flicker upward. "I'm sorry I gave away our news prematurely."

He wrapped me in an unexpected hug. "We'll stop buying bacon for a while."

That made me laugh. "Least of our problems." I sobered. "Go to your daughter. She needs you. I'm a big girl...soon to get bigger."

"I don't think Sam wants me anywhere near her right now, but I do need to get her to school. Will you be okay? Do you need to stay home?"

I soaked in his care and concern, letting myself relax into his chest for a moment. I could take care of myself. But damn did it feel amazing to have Chance's support. Even more so because he had a very pressing problem waiting for him in his SUV.

"Physically I feel a lot better," I told him. "My stomach just needed to empty itself. I'll be at work." I nearly asked him if he was doing okay, but I knew he wasn't, so I held the question in. "We'll get her through this, Chance."

"Keep telling me that." He kissed my forehead, then ended the hug. "See you at work."

Chapter Twenty-Three

Chance

By the time I got home from work, it was nearly six thirty p.m. My daughter hadn't come home from school yet, but she *had* deigned to send me a curt message saying she was at Kinsley's house.

I was pulling out the ingredients for homemade chicken tortilla soup when Rowan came down the stairs and into the kitchen.

"Welcome home," she said. She'd changed from work clothes into leggings and a sweatshirt, and her hair was tousled. Her feet were bare, her toenails painted a deep navy blue. She looked adorably sleepy. I couldn't help imagining what it would be like to be able to crawl into bed next to her and pull her into my body for a late-afternoon snooze...and maybe more. If I were in bed with her, definitely more.

I shook off the inappropriate thoughts, turned back to the counter, and slid the cutting board toward me. I turned on the heat under the big soup pot. "Did you get a nap?"

She'd looked about to drop by late afternoon, so I'd suggested she go home early and rest. That she'd taken my suggestion to leave work told me how exhausted she must've been.

"I passed out. Thanks again for letting me leave early, boss."

"Not your boss," I said, smiling in spite of my mood.

"Is Sam home yet?"

My smile dropped. I took out the carrots and began slicing them in an even, therapeutic rhythm. "She went to Kinsley's house. I checked her phone's location and verified it."

"That's the girl who befriended her when you first moved to town, right?"

"That's right. They haven't gotten together for months."

"She told me about her when we were baking. Kinsley's not one of the mean girls?"

I shook my head.

"This is a positive thing," Rowan said.

"She's avoiding home and me. How is that positive?"

Rowan touched my shoulder. She pulled her hand away too soon for my liking. "She has a lot to sort through. She's found a friend to help her."

I'd been admittedly too upset to consider that truth until now. "If I remember right, Kinsley has a really young sibling, like two or three years old. So maybe there's some common ground there. Parents too old to be having babies."

"Thirty-six is not too old," Rowan said with a half laugh. "What can I do to help with dinner? Onions?" She gestured to the one I'd set out.

"Sure." I handed her a second knife and cutting board. "Thirty-six is a lot older than you."

"Seven years? That's nothing."

"I'm glad you see it that way," I said. "My daughter probably sees it as her old man knocked up a girl in her twenties."

"Stop, Chance. Sam is probably more concerned about how a baby will affect *her* life. You know how teenagers are."

"Everything revolves around them."

"Spot on. I won't pretend to know your daughter well, but if she's like other fourteen-year-olds, she hasn't stopped to think how this could be affecting *you* emotionally."

"Right." I considered that as I added oil to the hot pan. "I did the same thing—defaulted to my own feelings, I guess."

"Of course you did. That's what we humans do," she said as she chopped the onion.

"I need to dad up. Think about what she's going through. Damn." I seemed to be fucking up as a parent repeatedly. "I appreciate having your perspective. It helps. You seem able to understand my daughter better than I can, and you just met her."

"She's not my daughter. It's easier from the outside," she said modestly. She set the bowl of diced onion next to the stove for me. "What else can I do?"

I remembered the cornbread mix in the pantry and turned on the oven. "If you mix the cornbread, I'll get the rest of the soup ingredients ready."

"Deal."

As I cut the chicken and she mixed the bread ingredients, I said, "How do you think I should handle Sam not coming home after school?"

"Did she break a rule?"

"Not exactly, since she let me know where she was going."

"But she usually comes home."

"Lately she has." I tossed the last of the chicken into the pot. "She didn't when she was hanging out with Lacey and company."

"The mean girls?"

"The bad influences, we'll call them."

"But Kinsley's different."

"She seems to be. She hasn't been caught drinking on the beach with boys to my knowledge."

"Excellent," Rowan said with a touch of humor. "Today had to be rough on Sam. The pregnancy is huge, and the way she found out didn't help. Did she say when she'd be home?"

"'Later.'" I mimicked my teenager's defiance as I added seasonings and the rest of the ingredients to the pot.

"I'd say as long as she comes home at a decent hour, let it go. You have other battles to fight."

I nodded as everything she said clicked into place in my head. "You make a lot of sense."

"There'll be friction with her about my pregnancy for who knows how long. If it were my kid, I think I'd cut her slack on things like going to a friend's unless she breaks a rule or outwardly defies you. But she's not my kid, and I don't know anything about parenting, so..."

"Nobody knows anything about parenting." It came out sounding flippant, but I meant every word. "In my dads' group, everyone says the same thing. Even West, who has three kids... He says none of them are the same, not even his twins, so you never feel like you know what you're doing."

"I'm hoping you have some baby basics down for this one," she said, pointing at her middle. "It's been a lot of years since I changed a diaper, back when I babysat as a teenager."

"Which was probably about the same time Sam was in diapers, so it's been just as long for me." I'd said it as a joke, but as I ran the math, I realized it was likely true.

"Good thing we decided to co-parent, huh?"

Her tone was lighthearted, but mine went serious when I said, "Doing it alone is not a picnic."

Rowan came forward with the baking dish ready to go in the oven. I stepped out of her way so she could put it in. When she straightened, she sought eye contact and put a hand on my arm.

"Chance, I think you're doing okay with Sam. There might be bobbles, as there is with literally every single teenager on the planet, but you've instilled good stuff in her. Whatever you've been doing, she's got a solid foundation. I can tell."

"Most days it doesn't feel good enough."

"It *is* good enough. I'm sure she's had a shit show of a day, but deep down, she knows you love her."

I hoped like hell that was true. Who ever fucking knew?

What I did know was that it was damn nice to have someone to talk to about it. Someone who reassured me, seemingly genuinely.

Sure, I had the dad group, but I saw them less often than I used to, and half the time, we spent our evenings talking about anything *but* our kids.

Another thing that was damn nice was spending time with Rowan. Having another adult to talk to not only about Sam but about anything. A friendly conversationalist who didn't make me doubt every word I said, wondering if it would be the wrong thing.

"Thanks for helping with dinner," I said a little later as we sat down with our soup and a plate piled high with steaming cornbread.

"I'm happy to. Especially on days when I get a short power nap beforehand."

"You had a hell of a morning between throwing up your guts and then the Sam stuff."

"We both did," she said.

We were nearly finished with our food when I heard the garage door going up.

"She's home," I said.

"Deep breath. You got this."

The door to the house opened, then shut, and Sam appeared on the other side of the kitchen.

"Hey, Sammy."

"Hi, Sam," Rowan said.

"Hey," my daughter said begrudgingly. She paused with her hand on the knob of the basement door, coat still on, backpack over one shoulder.

"There's plenty of soup. Would you like some?" I asked.

"I ate at Kinsley's."

I set down my spoon, giving my daughter my full attention. "Do you want to sit and talk?"

"There's not really anything more to talk about, is there?" There was a thread of hurt in her voice.

"There's whatever you want to talk about."

Sam shrugged. "I've got homework to do."

"Okay. First, I've got something to say. I understand this is hard for you. I don't know how our lives will look in a few months, but you're very much at the heart of the decisions I make. I love you, Sam, and I'm sorry you're hurting."

Her eyes looked watery as she nodded. She didn't say a word, but I didn't detect anger like this morning. This was more sad, confused, concerned.

No anger seemed like a step in the right direction.

"Can I go now?" she asked tiredly.

"Yes. Good night, Sammy."

My daughter headed downstairs without another word. My chest ached for all the hurt I was causing her.

I stood and picked up my plate and bowl. Rowan did the same.

"That went better than this morning," she said quietly.

My jaw was clenched hard, so I merely nodded once as I carried everything to the kitchen and set it down. I braced my arms on the counter, hating that my daughter was hurting yet again. Hating even more that I was the cause of it.

"Chance."

Rowan tugged at my arm and pulled me toward her. She wrapped her arms around me, our bodies flush, her sweet scent enveloping me. Softening my frustration. Calming me.

I hugged her back, holding her close. I closed my eyes and breathed her in.

"Thank you," I whispered into her hair.

"She might be *your* daughter, but I'm in this with you. Whatever you need. Whatever she needs. Whatever she'll let me do."

My chest lightened with gratitude, and my throat felt clogged with emotions, so I merely nodded and pulled her closer.

I might've made my life a mess, but there wasn't anyone I'd rather be in this mess with than this woman.

Chapter Twenty-Four

Rowan

For better or worse, I was beginning to feel at home in Chance's house. At home for now, maybe? Who knew where I'd land in the future or what my life would look like? I tried not to worry about it. One thing at a time, my grandmother would've told me.

That one thing at this moment was lasagna, baking in the oven, smelling like heaven and memories.

Chance was out with his dad group for the evening. Sam was in the basement. I'd worked up the guts and the energy to attempt Gram's lasagna recipe—cut in half—for the first time by myself. I'd helped her plenty of times growing up. I had memories of standing on a kitchen chair so I could reach the counter, layering the cooked noodles over the other ingredients.

The last time Gram had cooked homemade lasagna for me was my twenty-third birthday. As we'd taken our first few bites, she'd realized she'd forgotten to add the garlic, and we'd laughed and laughed. Looking back now, with twenty-twenty hindsight, I was sure that'd been an early sign of her dementia, though we'd had no idea what had been ahead of us then.

Not knowing was probably a blessing.

I realized I had a sad smile on my face as I stood against the kitchen cabinet thinking about her. I chose to cling to the laughter part of the memory. The love. Not the early stages of disease or the beginning of the end.

Footsteps on the stairs jolted me to the present. The basement door swung open, and Sam peered at me from the top step.

"What is that incredible smell?" she asked, then entered the kitchen.

I smiled, surprised at her appearance and warmed by her compliment. "I'm attempting my grandmother's lasagna recipe."

"If it tastes like it smells, it's a really good recipe."

The one thing I was sure of was that I remembered the garlic. "You're helping me eat it, right?"

Her expression was a mix of shyness and eagerness as she asked, "You have enough to share?"

I went to the oven and opened it a crack to show her a small baking dish of Italian splendor. "I have enough. I hope it doesn't suck." I shut the oven to let it bake another couple of minutes.

"My dad will be sad he missed this. Lasagna is his favorite."

I found it telling she thought of her dad so readily. Chance might think his daughter hated him, but that said otherwise.

"If it tastes okay, maybe I'll make a full batch one of these days," I said. "This was a test run. I didn't want to spend hours making it for you guys and have it not turn out."

The timer went off. I ended it and grabbed the oven mitts.

Sam took two plates from the cabinet as I pulled the bubbling pan out of the oven and set it on the stove.

The lasagna pan was hot, so we scooped up servings at the stove. I wondered if Sam would retreat to the basement with her food, but she didn't. She sat at the table with me, and we dug in to our dinner—which incidentally tasted just like Gram's, the garlic version. If I closed my eyes, I could imagine my grandmother at the table with us.

"This is delicious. It's your grandma's recipe?" Sam asked.

"Yeah. We made it together when I was a kid, but I haven't tried it solo."

Sam watched me, then tilted her head and said, "Is she...?"

"She died in December."

"I'm sorry," Sam said. She brushed stray strands of her hair behind her ear, then forked another bite. "That's so recent."

"Yeah." I forced a bittersweet smile. "In some ways it seems like last week, but also, it feels like an eternity since I've hugged her."

"It's been years since I could hug my mom."

"I bet you still miss her," I said carefully. I acted as if this was normal for us, trying to seem low-key and nonchalant even as I was encouraged and hopeful at the chance to connect.

"Yeah. Sometimes."

"I still miss my mom, and she died when I was seven."

"That's a long time. I was six, so almost the same age."

"We'll always miss our moms, huh?" I said, watching her for cues whether this was too tough of a subject. Chance had mentioned both he and Sam had gone to grief counseling years ago, but that didn't mean talking about her mom would ever be easy.

"Mine was...different." Sam bit her lip and averted her gaze. "She was an addict."

"Your dad told me a little about her. That's a lot to sort through."

"I think of it like an illness," she said, taking me aback with her wisdom.

"Yes. Addiction is a type of illness."

"A really ugly one."

I nodded, wondering how much of Erin's downward slide Sam had been witness to. "But she was your mom, and you loved her," I said. "It's hard to grow up without a mom."

"You did too, huh?"

I nodded. "And a dad."

"What?" she exclaimed. "Your dad died too?"

"They were in a helicopter crash."

"Oh, my God. That's terrible."

"Yeah. But my grandparents took me in and raised me. I was lucky to have them."

"I'm lucky to have my dad," she said as if she hadn't considered the possibility of losing both parents before. "Even if we aren't very close anymore."

"I've sensed that," I fudged. "Is there a reason?"

She stuck a bite of lasagna in her mouth and looked pensive as she chewed. "I don't know," she finally said. "It's just...awkward. Like, he doesn't get what it's like to be a girl, you know?" She picked up her water glass and took a drink.

"Like periods and boys?"

"Yessss." Sam set her glass down with emphasis. "I

mean, he had *the talk* with me a few years ago. It was mortifying."

I let out a grin. "Probably for him too?"

"He seemed embarrassed. Short and to the point."

"I've never had to give the talk, but I'm sure it's a tough one."

She shoveled another bite in with a frown, giving me the impression she was holding back something she wanted to say.

I continued eating and waited to see if she'd say more.

After two bites and another drink, she did. "It made me really miss my mom in a way. Or *a* mom, because I didn't really get a chance to know my mom very well as a person. Just...it'd be easier with a mom, I think."

"Right. Someone who lives with girl stuff every day."

"Yes," she said more confidently. "Like, my dad doesn't know about cramps or what to do if a tampon leaks."

I made a cringing face and tried to imagine if my grandfather had been in charge of the talk. *Thank God for Gram.*

"And boys... The one time he got me to admit I had a crush on someone, he told me I'm too young and I should forget boys until I'm thirty."

I held in a laugh. *I* knew that was Chance being a protective, loving father, but I could see how that might not land right from Sam's perspective.

I pressed my lips together and pondered what to say. "Dads don't want their daughters to get hurt. Ever. But that was a total dad comment. I can see why it would make it hard to talk to him about boys."

"Not hard. Impossible. I messed up and told him Cody Billings tried to get me to drink beer, and my dad got this look in his eyes like he wanted to murder Cody. Which honestly I would support because Cody is a creep and a jerk."

"There *are* a lot of those in high school," I said.

"Tons of them," she agreed.

I set my fork down and took a drink, figuring out so much about this father-daughter relationship in just a few short minutes. Maybe I could help Chance understand how he came across without betraying Sam's confidence. I didn't want to be in the middle, but I wanted them to have a better relationship.

As I put my glass down, I said, "The one thing I know for certain is that your dad loves you a lot. He might bumble like boys do, but you're the most important person in his life."

"Now he'll have two kids," Sam said evenly. "I was pissed at him when I found out about you being pregnant."

"That must've been really hard to hear. I will say this. Your dad's biggest concern the whole time I've known him is you. He loves you to the moon and back."

"I know." She scraped melted cheese off her plate with her fork.

"It's still okay to be mad," I said. "Your emotions are your emotions."

"I don't think I'm mad anymore."

"Yeah?" I asked, encouraged but afraid to say the wrong thing.

"Kinsley and I have talked a lot. *A lot*."

"Girlfriends are the best," I said.

"Her little sister is barely two, and she's adorable. Kinsley loves being a big sister and—" She whipped her head toward me. "Wait. Will I be able to be in your baby's life?"

"I was hoping you'd want to be," I said. "You'll be family."

She seemed to consider that as she continued to focus on cheese scraping.

"I don't have any family left," I continued. "I'd love my baby to have a big sister like you."

"We'd make a weird family."

"Unconventional," I corrected. "Different, but who cares? Family's everything, whether it's blood family or found family."

"Found family." She nodded pensively. "I like that. It's really only my dad and me. My mom's parents died before I was born, and my dad's parents... We don't talk to them very often."

I so didn't understand that whole dynamic, but if Chance's parents were too blind to see what a wonderful person their son was, that was their loss. And how could they not want to know their granddaughter better?

"That's too bad," I said.

She shrugged. "I figure if they don't want to be in our lives, we're better off without them."

"It's their loss."

"It's sad that your grandma won't meet your baby. She sounds like the type who'd be excited about a great-grandkid."

"She would've loved this baby so much." I put my hand on my belly, my eyes tearing at the thought.

"I'm sorry," Sam said. "I didn't mean to make you sad."

I shook my head and dabbed at the corners of my eyes with my napkin. "You didn't. I think about her every day. I can still hear her voice in my head, from the years before dementia got to her, when she was clear and her voice was strong. Sometimes I can almost *feel* the love she'd have for my baby, as if it's a tangible thing." I shook my head. "I'm sure that doesn't make sense."

"It's like she's watching over you," Sam said with incredible insight for her age. But then she had firsthand experience with a loved one's death.

"Sometimes I could swear she is," I said. "I went into that yarn place downtown a couple weeks ago—"

"Fat Cat."

"Right. I went in to avoid that llama that apparently sneaks out to go to the bakery?"

"Esmerelda."

I laughed. "Everybody knows this llama. Anyway, I didn't set out to go to Fat Cat, but once I was in there, surrounded by all that yarn, I felt Gram's presence. She loved to knit. I found some beautiful yarn, and long story short, Loretta, the owner, offered to help me knit a baby blanket. I'm going tomorrow for my first lesson. Or re-lesson? My Gram taught me, but let's just say I'm not a natural."

"Do you think... Would you mind if I went with you? I want to learn to knit."

I tried not to show how happy her question made me. Because teenagers and enthusiasm... There were limits, and this was new. Sam and I were new. "You absolutely can come. I'd love to have a knitting buddy."

"Maybe I can learn to make adorable little sweaters for the baby."

"That would be amazing," I said, with visions of the cutest handmade baby clothes filling my head. "Likely way over my sad capabilities, but you... I have every bit of confidence Loretta could teach you how."

"Annika, Kinsley's sister, was wearing this adorable

striped sweater the other day: pink, yellow, and cream. I want to make something like that."

"We'd have the best-dressed baby in town."

As we split the last portion of lasagna, we kept talking, turning to lighter topics, everything from her classes to her newish friendship with Kinsley to why I became a teacher. We bonded over Taylor Swift songs, home science experiments, and cute socks.

So much about my future was uncertain, looming, scary. My life was one big question mark after another. Where would I end up living? Would I eventually get back into teaching? How would Chance and I manage co-parenting? Would we ever share more than kisses and a kid? How soon would I have to break down and buy pants with a bigger waist? And most importantly, how would I handle having a little human dependent on me?

All of it circled through my brain at different moments throughout the day. All of it could stress me out in a heartbeat.

But these forty-five minutes with Sam, just the two of us getting to know each other better? It gave me hope and made it easier to believe maybe everything would end up all right.

Chapter Twenty-Five

Chance

One of the cool things about having a former NFL quarterback in our dad group was that Max could afford man toys and liked to share.

He'd recently outfitted the walkout basement of his lakefront home with a pool table, a foosball table, and a video game system like nothing I'd ever seen that put thousands of games at our fingertips, from 80s Galaga and Donkey Kong to the latest console games.

Harper, his fiancée, had taken two-year-old Danny for a sleepover at her apartment with Dakota so Max could host us this week. All five of the rest of us had shown up—Knox, Ben, Luke, West, and me—and we'd gravitated toward some cutthroat foosball and pool first thing.

Max had smoked a shit ton of ribs, made a slow cooker full of baked beans, mixed two pans of corn bread, and stirred up some cole slaw just like a regular Martha Stewart. Between the food and the toys, it was no wonder his house was our favorite place to meet.

After our initial breaking-in of the game tables, we sat around in his basement that felt more like a high-class men's club, minus naked women, stuffing the damn good food in our faces and shooting the shit.

"So Danny's hanging out with the pretty girls tonight, huh?" West said as he leaned over a rib.

"If by pretty girls you mean his future mommy and her friend," Max said. "We started the adoption process last week. It should be official shortly after the wedding."

"Congrats on getting it started," Ben said. "We're going through that times two. Or four, depending on how you look at it."

"There's gonna be an awful lot of little Holloways running around this town," Luke said.

"That's just the four they've already got," West joked. "How long till you and Emerson increase that population yet again?"

"We're not in any hurry," Ben said. "We both remember how much work infants and toddlers are."

"Nothing quite like potty training," West agreed, shaking his head. "I've heard boys are easier."

"Built-in target shooting," Luke said. "Addie was pretty easy. Just had to bribe her with Skittles, and she was all over it."

"I suspect Danny's gonna be a project," Max said. "His latest trick is stripping down naked and streaking around the house—or my mom's house if he happens to be there."

"Naked?" I asked. "Diaper and everything?"

"Diaper and everything." Max laughed. "I haven't found any good advice on parenting sites for this one."

"Maybe potty training will be easy with him," Knox said. "Could he be ready now? Just throw him on the toilet every time he gets naked?"

"He's barely two, but it's worth a try," Max said, eyebrows raised.

"Juniper's got a while before we start," Knox said. "We've currently got our hands full with tantrums."

"She's not even two yet, is she?" I asked.

Knox shook his head. "She'll be two in May."

"You got a precocious one there," West said.

Knox held up his bottle of Rusty Anchor. "I'm very afraid of my future."

We all laughed—*with* him, not *at* him. We each knew our time would come for all the "fun" stages. I'd always thought I was done with the infant and toddler ones and taunted these guys with teenage ones. The joke was on me apparently, though none of them knew it yet except for West.

I got up for more ribs and a handful of paper towels, knowing I needed to tell them my news but unsure how to start.

Someone's phone rang.

"Hell," Ben said as he wiped sauce off his hands. "I'd rather not have an emergency tonight."

As the town vet, he'd had his evenings out interrupted plenty of times before.

"It's Emerson," he said when he saw the screen, relaxing and accepting the call. "Hey, Ems."

I carried my plate back to the table where we were eating. Either we were all nosy or just busy stuffing our faces because no one except Ben spoke, allowing us to hear his conversation.

"What do you mean Esmerelda won't let you into the stall?" he asked his wife.

Emerson was emphatic and emotional on the other end, loud enough we could get the idea there were llama shenanigans, even though we couldn't quite understand her words.

"Just another day at the Holloway house," Knox joked.

"You're sure it's not one of the barn cats?" Ben said into the phone.

"Only a couple dozen of those to keep track of," Max said, grinning.

"It's not Pixie, is it?... Ah. Right." Ben stood and took several aimless steps away from the table. "Can you get Esmerelda out of her stall?"

"Things must be desperate if he thinks letting that llama out would be a good thing," Max said.

The five of us not on the call cracked llama jokes and brought up some of Esmerelda's previous stunts. Max had helped capture her multiple times and probably deserved some kind of honorary veterinary designation. Llama capture specialist?

"I have to go," Ben said to us as he came back to the table. "As soon as I finish my beans and this last rib." He sat back down and spooned in some beans as we waited.

"The escape artist llama won't come out of her stall now?" Knox asked.

"It seems Esmerelda is adding protective services to her llama resume," Ben said between bites. "A stray cat got into her stall and is curled up in the back corner. Emerson suspects the cat has an injured leg, but she can't be sure, because Esmerelda won't let anyone get close to the cat."

"She's not planning to eat the cat, is she?" Max asked with a chuckle.

"She's a vegetarian." Ben finished his beans, as unbothered as could be. "Emerson tried to slip past Esmerelda, and the llama spit at her. My wife is threatening to make llama sausage."

That spurred laughter all around. Emerson might talk tough, but she'd never hurt her husband's beloved llama.

Once Ben had stuffed his food down the gullet, he stood, took care of his plate, and said, "I'm off to battle the beasts and see if I can help a stray cat."

"That one'll end up adopted," Max said to the rest of us. "You watch."

"You're a cat household now," Ben said to him, pointing at the duo of kittens asleep in the center of the pool table while we took a break from it. "I'll get Harper on my side, and soon you'll have three instead of two felines."

"Not gonna happen," Max called out to him.

Ben left, and the rest of us joked about his situation while we finished eating.

I needed to spill my news soon. Once the food was cleaned up, they planned to go into video game mode, and my chance would be lost. I wanted these guys to know before word got out all over town. Now that Sam knew, it was a matter of time.

"So," I said, standing at the bar where the food had been served. "Before the games begin, I've got something to say."

West already knew everything, and he seemed to sense that's where I was going. For once he didn't crack any smart-ass comments. He stood next to me, as if in support. I nodded at him in thanks.

"What's going on?" Knox asked as he tossed some trash in the waste basket.

You'd think I'd have a plan for what to say, but I still hadn't figured it out. To hell with easy. I opted for blunt.

"I'm going to be a father again," I said.

All movement in the room halted as three heads turned my way. I saw West nod out of the corner of my eye.

"I don't know which question to ask first," Luke said.

"You got a girl pregnant?" Max asked.

"I'm not planning to give birth myself," I said dryly.

"Who?" Knox asked.

"What the fuck?" was Luke's question.

"Did you know about this?" Max asked West. "You must have for you to be able to keep quiet right now."

"Fucker," West said to him with a grin. "I knew."

"Your roommate hasn't been there long enough for you to get her with child, has she?" Luke came up on the other side of me and stopped, looking like he was doing math in his head.

"The timing is suspect," Max said.

"You gonna put them out of their misery?" West asked me.

"Once they shut up and listen," I told him lightly.

"I'm listening." Knox stood on the opposite side of the bar, his attention fully on me.

"I hooked up with someone on New Year's Eve," I said.

"It was your roommate," Knox said, sounding sure of it. He'd been at the inn's party.

"Was it?" Luke popped the lid off another beer.

"She wasn't my roommate then, but yes. It's Rowan. The night we got together, I thought she was just in town for a short stay. She ended up getting a job from Chloe."

"At the brewery?" Luke asked.

"What are the chances?" Max said.

"Chloe and Rowan have a friend in common," I explained. "But I didn't know any of that until Rowan's first day on the job."

I explained how I hadn't seen her since our hookup and hadn't expected to ever see her again. How we'd then agreed we could work together without a problem.

"And then she found out she was pregnant," I said.

"Shit." Luke stared at me with his beer halfway to his mouth.

"That was pretty much my thought too," I said.

Max reached to the upper cabinets and took out a bottle of whiskey.

"Good call, amigo," West said as our host distributed highball glasses and filled them with the top-shelf liquor.

"So now Rowan's living with you?" Knox asked. "You didn't mention you were involved with someone."

"I'm not," I said. "Ben would appreciate this part of the story. Rowan was having a hard time finding a place to live, so I told her I had a spare room. She eventually agreed. We just told Sam about the baby a few days ago, so the secret's out now. I wanted you guys to hear it from me, not the Tattler."

"Shit," Luke said again. "How're you doing with this?"

"I'll let you know when I figure that out." I rubbed the back of my neck, trying to release the tension.

"But you and Rowan aren't involved?" Knox asked.

"That depends on how you define involved," West said. "If you're living together and having a baby together, you're involved."

"But not romantically," I said emphatically. I raised my glass to my lips and swigged the whiskey.

"She's not the type you'd want to have a relationship with?" Max asked.

I took a few seconds to find the right words. "If I was open to a relationship, Rowan would be the type I'd want."

"Why aren't you open to a relationship?" The expression on Luke's face said he thought I was a dumbass.

Letting myself get further involved with Rowan would be the true dumbass move.

"We're planning to share parenting duties," I said.

"That's eighteen plus years. We don't know quite how it'll look, but I don't want to do anything to fuck up that co-parent relationship."

"Who's to say it would fuck it up?" Knox asked.

"What are the chances this woman I spent less than one night with and I could make it work for the long run?" I countered.

"But what if you could?" Luke asked. "There's a risk, sure, but there's also a big potential payoff if you make it work. That baby would be better off with a real, cohesive family than some kind of shared custody arrangement. A mom and a dad, a sister, a stable home."

"That's true," Knox said.

That thought had done more than cross my mind. It'd gotten in and camped out, making it harder to know which was the bigger risk and what would be better for the kids.

"You have to look at the other side too," West said to the others. "What happens if they make a go of it and it doesn't work out? The kid loses."

"You're coming from a string of relationships that didn't work out," Luke said to West. "No offense, man."

"None taken. My track record's shit," West said with a humble chuckle. "Which is why I won't get serious with anyone anymore. Chance is smart to keep his heart out of it."

"Chance's history is different from yours," Luke pointed out. "He's been married once. No breakups. Just a tragic end."

"That tragic end fucked with my head," I said honestly. "I know Erin was an addict, but what if *I* was what made her so unhappy she needed to numb herself?"

"I thought you said she got hooked after a medical procedure," Max said.

I shrugged. "Who really knows? I don't know how long she was on the pills. Did she start them because of physical pain like I thought? Was she already hooked when I met her? Addicts hide shit. She never came up to me and said, *honey, I think I took one too many pills, and now I can't stop.*"

"I can't imagine what you went through," Knox said, "but Erin has nothing to do with Rowan and your current situation."

"If there's some chemistry, maybe you two should give it a go," Luke said. "See what happens instead of jumping ten steps ahead and assuming it'll be a breakup."

"I get what you guys are saying." I took another big gulp, let the alcohol sit on my tongue, then swallowed it, savoring that burn. I couldn't pretend there was no chemistry between Rowan and me. It was all I could do not to repeat that kiss that never should've happened.

Fuck. Giving in to the attraction was tempting twenty-four seven. Was I being a dumbass to straight up rule it out? Or would it be the worst move ever to try to make it work with Rowan?

"My confidence in interpersonal relationships is in the shitter," I told them. "I have enough trouble with Sam, and now I'll be throwing a baby into the mix. How dumb would it be to add a woman?"

"They come with some upsides." Knox held up his glass for a toast, grinning. "Here's to sex on the regular."

"Oh, see, this is where we draw the line. It should be three against two," West said, "the singles who have to work for it versus you married and engaged fuckers. But we got romantic Luke over there who's a unicorn and gets along with his baby mama to this day."

"It doesn't have to be contentious," Luke said.

Luke and Addie's mom had never been married. Their relationship had been brief, from what I understood. Now the mom was in the military. Luke had full-time custody, but he let Addie's mom spend as much time with the girl as she could whenever she was on leave.

"Not everyone can get along like you and what's-her-name," West said.

"Do you really want to be single and lonely for the rest of your life?" Luke asked, his gaze zeroing in on me.

After Erin's death, I'd convinced myself I wanted to be single for as long as it took to get Sam raised. I hadn't accounted for meeting someone like Rowan.

"Truth?" I said, swirling my nearly empty glass. "I don't know what the hell I want."

I'd expected these guys to side with me, to have my back and easily see I had my hands full with a teenager and, soon, a baby. I'd thought they'd consider my decision to keep distance between Rowan and me a wise one.

I should've known better. Half our group was blissfully in love and forgot how rocky it was to start a new relationship and build it into something solid. They were there, on solid ground.

The thing was, the more I saw how happy my turncoat friends were, the more I started to want what they had for myself.

I needed to keep my wits about me and my dick in my pants until I figured out what was best, not only for me but for everyone involved.

Chapter Twenty-Six

Chance

The following Saturday night, circumstances lined up for me to treat Rowan to some fun that had nothing to do with work or babies.

Sam was at Kinsley's for a sleepover, and this time my talk with her dad was trust-inspiring instead of the hints of concern I'd experienced on New Year's Eve with Lacey's mom. Rowan had napped before dinner, so she was more likely to have energy for an evening out. And I had insider info on a downtown event Rowan would love.

As we climbed into my SUV after dinner at home, it almost felt like a date, except it wasn't. We weren't carefree singles. We weren't exploring a harmless attraction. We were expectant parents with a truckload of challenges to navigate. But I was ready to help her set the tough stuff aside for a few hours.

"Now are you going to tell me where you're taking me?" Rowan asked as I backed out of the driveway.

"Not far," was all I said, grinning because I knew that wasn't what she was looking for.

"You're mean. I'm not good with surprises." She pretended to pout.

"I'm learning that." I laughed. "Can you trust me?"

She eyed me across the front seat, dark except for when we passed under a streetlight. "I don't know. Can I?"

"Of course." When we hit Main, I turned toward downtown. "We're going to the Fly."

"That's next to Humble's, right?"

"Right."

"So we're going to a bar? Are you planning to get your pregnant roommate roaring drunk or...?" She left the nonserious question hanging.

I laughed again. "Last time we drank together, it was life-changing."

"True story," she said, laughing with me. "It's a good thing I won't be drinking tonight."

I didn't even try to find a parking spot on the square. I could see from a couple of blocks away, traffic was backed up, and there were people everywhere, which wasn't surprising. It was early March, and the weather had been springlike all day, luring the people of Dragonfly Lake outside in droves.

"I'll have to park on a side street a few blocks away," I told her. "Do you want me to drop you off at the door?"

"I can walk. I need to walk. Especially after that delicious dinner."

"It was just enchiladas. Nothing special."

"Someone cooking my dinner while I napped? I felt like a spoiled princess. Of course, now I know you were scheming to get me out of the house."

"Busted. You must be tired of sitting at home every

night though." I found a parking spot along the curb on a side street about a block from Main.

Rowan and I had been cooking together most evenings, then hanging out until bedtime. But today, on our day off from work, I'd taken pleasure in giving her extra time to relax.

"Generally speaking, I'm just plain tired," she said. "But depending on what we're doing tonight, it might be fun to get out. If only I knew what that was..."

I killed the engine, got out of the car, and strode around to Rowan's door.

"You want the surprise spoiled?" I asked when I opened her door.

"Yes, please."

I offered my hand to help her out, pretending I was only assisting her because she was pregnant and not because I liked to touch her. "You're a fan of Everly Ash, right?"

"I was even before I lived in the same small town as her," Rowan said of the country singer once she was next to me on the sidewalk.

"She's doing a pop-up acoustic show at the Fly."

Rowan whipped her head toward me, her mouth open, her brows raised. "Really?"

"I wouldn't make that up," I said with a laugh.

Everly had made headlines as the Nashville country starlet turned runaway bride around the time Sam and I had moved to Dragonfly Lake. Long story short, she was now married to Holden's brother Seth and had taken her career indie. Her impromptu performances around town were crowd-pleasers.

"Oh! This is exciting. Is the Fly very big?"

"It's big for a bar, but not for a concert. They don't often have live music."

"How do you know about it if it's a pop-up?"

I peered down at her.

"Oh," she said, answering herself. "Because she's Holden and Chloe's sister-in-law."

"Bingo."

"So no one else knows?"

I checked the time on my phone. Nearly seven p.m. Everly was starting around 7:30, before the big Saturday-night rush of twentysomethings hit the bars. "I'm sure some people do. Her friends and family. It wasn't advertised though."

As we reached Main Street, the scene was even more chaotic than I expected. Sheriff Lopez was directing traffic, and people had gathered in front of the bakery.

I let out a howl of laughter.

"What is going on?" Rowan asked in alarm.

"Looks like we got a llama on the loose," I said. "See that van over there?" I pointed across from the bakery at the older-model van. Emerson had hired Lexie North, another of Holden's sisters-in-law, to paint a giant portrait of Esmerelda and Betty on the side, as well as the word Llamamobile in a fancy script.

"Llamamobile," Rowan read. "You have got to be kidding me. This is the oddest town ever."

"Where else is the second-most-famous resident a furry white llama?"

"Nowhere," she said, laughing. "Where's the llama?"

As we got closer to the scene, I spotted Ben coming from the back of the van after shutting the llama hatch.

"It looks like they just got her loaded up."

"This is my second near miss. I've never officially met this llama, only dodged her."

"Hey, I've got connections. Come on." I took Rowan's

hand and headed into the street that was now deserted of cars except for the sheriff's and the llama van.

"She's in the van?" Rowan asked. "I'm not going in that van with her."

"We'll say hi from outside." As we neared the van, I called out to Ben, "When are you going to get that llama under control?"

Standing at his open driver's door, Ben shook his head. "This fucking llama. I can't for the life of me figure out how she gets out. I've fixed multiple spots in the fence. Every time I think I've got it, I get a call that she's out and about. Hi," he said to Rowan, holding out his hand. "Ben Holloway."

"Rowan Andrews. Nice to meet you."

"She wants to meet the llama," I explained to my friend. I leaned over to see into the passenger seat. "Hey, Emerson."

Ben's wife had just climbed in the other side. She stretched toward the driver's seat. "Hey, Chance. Would you like to *buy* a llama?" She grinned, then turned her attention to Rowan. "You must be Rowan." She leaned even farther, and the women shook hands.

I wondered if Ben had told her about Rowan or if our pregnancy news was filtering through town. On second thought, I was better off not knowing the details. I deliberately hadn't opened the Tattler app for the past week now that our secret was out.

"I am," Rowan said. "You're the llama mama?"

"I'm the wife of the llama softie," Emerson said, laughing with the rest of us. "I'm adopting Ben's human kids, but we haven't started proceedings for any of the furry creatures yet. This one is last on my list."

"What she means to say is that she loves this high-drama llama," Ben said. "Meet Esmerelda."

Rowan angled to better see the white llama, who was enclosed behind a mesh metal partition. The llama checked her out with her big, astute eyes, her ears angling forward in interest. "Hi, Esmerelda. Aren't you a pretty girl?"

"Or funny-looking, as our six-year-old says," Emerson said. "She kind of grows on you."

"The llama," Ben clarified. "The six-year-old is easier to love. What are you two up to tonight?"

"Heading to the Fly," I said.

"To see a certain someone who shall remain nameless?" Ben asked.

"Worst-kept secret, huh?"

"Chloe clued me in," Emerson said.

"But first we've gotta take care of the cookie fiend." Ben peered in at Esmerelda. "Yes, I mean you." His voice dripped with affection.

"Question of the hour," I said, "did she get a cookie?"

"How do you think we got her in the van?" Ben asked, laughing.

"If I ate as many cookies as she does, I'd weigh twice as much," Emerson said.

"At least she gets a workout walking to the bakery, huh?" I joked. "So you're taking her home, then coming to the Fly?"

"That's the plan," Ben said. "Bertie has the kids tonight, so we just need the animals to behave."

"We'll hope to see you there."

"Nice to meet you both," Rowan said.

Sheriff Lopez came toward the van. "You got her all tucked in?"

"Sure do. We'll get her out of here and locked in the

barn," Ben said. "Appreciate your help. Again. Sorry for the trouble. Again."

The sheriff laughed. "If Sugar's cookies weren't so good, I might not be so understanding."

"Blame it on Sugar." I grinned and nodded at the sheriff. "Good luck getting her home," I said to Ben as I ushered Rowan beyond the van.

It felt natural to put my arm around her and rest my hand on her waist as we headed down the sidewalk.

"I feel like I've earned official resident status now that I've met Esmerelda," Rowan said.

"You're one of us."

"It's crazy, but"—she peered up at me, looking invigorated and so damn pretty—"I sort of love it."

Affection and happiness shone in her coffee-brown eyes, making me wish for a moment those feelings were aimed at *me*. I knew I should shut down on thoughts like that, but I was tired of fighting them. Tonight felt special. We didn't have to guard our secret anymore, and so far Rowan was okay with me touching her in public. Why not just relax and savor this rare evening out together?

"Told you it's a special place," I said.

I opened the door to the Fly and kept my hand on her... possessively? Maybe. I wasn't okay with some other guy trying to win her affection. Obviously that was something I'd have to get over in the long run, but for tonight, she was here with me. Knowing she wasn't up for entanglements, I intended to stick close and provide a layer of protection from any assholes who thought they could win her over.

The bar wasn't crowded, as it was still a good two hours before people normally packed themselves in. That made it easy to spot Holden and Chloe, sitting at the bar in the front room, their backs to us.

Taking Rowan's hand, I led her toward them, weaving us between tables and people.

"Hello," I said, sticking my head between Holden and Chloe, who had an order of fries in front of them.

They both turned and greeted us. Chloe and Rowan hugged, and Rowan sat on the stool next to Chloe. They easily fell into conversation.

"Romantic night out, huh?" I teased Holden.

He laughed. "With a little one at home, you take what you can get. You might not remember what that's like, but you'll have a big refresher soon. Chloe didn't want to miss Everly."

"Where's Sutton tonight?"

"At her grandparents'. My dad and Faye's house has become like a weekend bed-and-breakfast service for the under-ten crowd. They love it."

"The kids or the grandparents?"

"Both," he said with a laugh. "They've got Mason and Eliza's three as well this evening, so Sutton's having cousin fun."

I'd met Mason and Eliza North a few times. The North family and the Henrys had become one big clan when Holden's sister, Hayden, had married Zane North, and then the Henry patriarch, Simon, and the North matriarch, Faye, had fallen in love and gotten hitched as well.

"You're lucky to have that kind of support," I said, unable to imagine what my life would've been like if my parents had ever doted on Sam.

I'd been so hopeful, when Erin was pregnant with our daughter, that my parents would be won over. It'd taken them nearly a week after we got home from the hospital to stop by and meet their only granddaughter. That lack of priority had finally drilled into my head that my parents truly didn't care.

"Faye and my dad are a godsend," Holden said.

"They're at seven minutes," Chloe announced excitedly, reading from a message on her phone.

"Ava's flirting with labor," Holden explained. "Contractions started a couple of hours ago."

"Cash is working tonight, trying to finish his shift before things get serious. Anna's with Ava, sending me updates," Chloe said.

"That's... I can't even imagine," Rowan said. "Terrifying? Exciting?"

"All the above," Chloe confirmed. "She's doing a home birth, so at least her husband won't have a chance to crash his car in a panic to get to the hospital." The look she sent Holden was full of both love and laughter.

"Top of the list for things I'll never live down," Holden said.

"You wrecked on the way to the hospital?" Rowan asked.

"Not exactly," he replied.

Chloe laughed. "It's worse." She explained how it'd been during Rusty Anchor's first evening event, where we'd highlighted some seasonal brews. She'd had contractions throughout the day and had pleaded with their unborn baby to give them a few more hours so Holden could finish the event.

"Baby didn't agree?" Rowan asked.

"Of course not. Sutton was stubborn even then. My water broke, so I had to tell Holden. He freaked out so much he put his precious car into gear instead of reverse and accelerated right into the concrete loading dock at the brewery."

I laughed even though I'd heard the story multiple times before.

Rowan's eyes went big, and she covered her mouth with her hand, holding in a laugh at the guy who signed her paycheck.

"Presley ended up driving us to the hospital for obvious reasons," Chloe said.

"Presley to the rescue," Rowan said.

"My brother only has to get from Henry's to their house behind the inn," Holden said. "Not even a mile."

"I can't believe he's working." I shook my head.

"Zinnia, the sous chef, had something in Nashville tonight," Chloe explained, "so he's at least trying to get through the dinner rush. So far their baby's going along with it." She checked the time on her phone again.

"Are you going over there to be with her?" Rowan asked.

"Ava decided just Cash and her midwife," Chloe said. "A private family thing, which I totally get. Even if I *will* be dying to see that baby!"

"They deserve their calm before the Henry-North storm, just like we had," Holden said.

"So true." Chloe pointed to an area against the wall, close to where we were. "There's Gin. She's Everly's producer. She's handling sound tonight."

It took less than ten minutes for Gin to set up a microphone, a stool, and some other equipment. As she worked, I pulled my phone out and checked Sam's location. When I saw she was exactly where she was supposed to be, I let out my breath. Maybe we'd turned a corner now that Lacey was out of the picture.

Everly made her way to the stool, introduced herself unnecessarily since everyone in town and most of the country knew who she was, and started singing and playing her guitar.

Within seconds, Rowan abandoned her stool and came to stand in front of me as the space filled up seemingly from nowhere with people gathering closer to Everly. Raphael, the manager of the Fly, stood to one side, ensuring people gave Everly plenty of space. Ben and Emerson joined us, only missing the first song.

A few songs in, Rowan leaned her back against me. Without thinking about it, I put my arms around her from behind, then kissed the top of her head. As soon as I did it, I wondered what the fuck I was doing. Trying to play it off, I kept my arms where they were and waited for any reaction from Rowan, holding my breath.

She turned her head to the side, and I thought she was going to say something. Instead she nuzzled it into my chest, just for a second, then rested her hand on one of mine.

Okay then. If she was okay with this, then so was I. So fucking okay.

Now that we weren't trying to hide her pregnancy, my guard was down. My body was confused. Or maybe my brain was, because actually, my body had a damn good idea of what it craved: the woman in my arms.

We remained entwined like that, with me more focused on Rowan than the music—her scent, the sway of her sexy hips to the beat, the way her body felt up against mine, as if it belonged there.

By about four songs in, I was hard as stone. I was sure Rowan could feel it. As she pressed even closer to me, she wove our fingers together. I took it as a good sign that she was as lost in the moment as I was.

Everly played for an hour. In the middle of her last song for the night, I leaned down to Rowan's ear.

"Are you ready to get out of here?" I asked her.

She met my gaze briefly, a sparkle in her eyes, and nodded.

With a wave toward Chloe, Holden, Ben, and Emerson, we headed through the throng of people toward the door, her hand in mine. I was so hard it hurt to walk.

When we got outside, I breathed in the brisk night air and tried to shake off the spell I'd been under from having my hands on Rowan for the past hour.

As we made our way down the sidewalk, she wove her arm through mine and held on.

"That was the coolest thing ever," she said. "Thank you, Chance."

"I thought you'd enjoy it. I did too. Her new songs are different. Better. Deeper."

"I read that one of the reasons she went indie was to write and sing what she wants. I still love her old stuff too, but I'd agree her new songs are even better."

We turned onto Main, which was llamaless and a lot less populated now that the bakery had closed and the diner was closing soon. As we walked by the yarn shop, Rowan slowed and peered in the display windows.

"Looking for your next project already?" I asked.

She scoffed. "I'll be lucky to get through one blanket before I'm fifty."

When she and Sam had come home from their knitting lesson last Sunday, my daughter had been bubbling over with enthusiasm for the scarf she'd started. Rowan had cracked jokes at her own expense, claiming she didn't apparently have the knitting gene. But she'd sung high praises to Loretta's patience and had sworn she was determined to finish her baby blanket.

"Our baby might need that blanket for his or her baby by then," I joked.

"I was looking for Purl, but surely Loretta takes the cat home at night?"

"I've seen photos on the Tattler. She has a modified baby buggy and wheels the cat the half block to her home each night."

Rowan laughed and snuggled closer to me.

When we reached my SUV, I helped her into the passenger side. I was reluctant to let go of her because I didn't know where the evening was heading, and I wasn't ready for it to be over. She seemed as into our connection as I was. We'd had multiple conversations about friends only, yet here we were, crossing lines.

Not only was my dating game fifteen years outdated, but our situation was unique. On top of all the gray areas in our "relationship" was the fact that Rowan was pregnant. Was it wrong to want to take your baby mama to bed?

As I went around to my side of the vehicle, the only thing I was sure about was that I didn't want our evening together to end yet.

Chapter Twenty-Seven

Rowan

By the time we pulled into the garage, my body was screaming for Chance's. I was pretty sure it had nothing to do with pregnancy hormones and everything to do with feeling his body against me for the past hour. His solid, *hard* body.

It went beyond knowing he was turned on...so far beyond that. I was beginning to suspect that, approximately three months ago when I'd landed somewhat randomly in Dragonfly Lake, decided on a whim to go to a New Year's Eve party, and said yes to the handsome stranger who'd asked me to dance, the universe had thrown me right in the path of the man who might be perfect for me.

We climbed out of the SUV without speaking, both of us apparently lost in our thoughts. Between Everly's music that resonated in my heart and Chance's closeness, I was buzzing with contentment.

When I'd moved into his house, I'd planned to stay in

my room most of the time, out of the way. I'd never intended to spend a lot of time with him or get to know him better. He'd been welcoming from the start though, including me in everything.

The better I knew Chance, the more I liked him. Whether we were cooking, working, or reading or watching a show together, living with him was comfortable. No, it was more than comfortable. I loved being with him.

Caring for my grandmother, I'd become such an island, a total loner. Of course she'd been there with me, but sadly she wasn't *really* there. Not the Gram I knew and loved. I'd figured out how to be alone with my thoughts, my fears, my decisions, because that's what she'd needed of me. I'd made it through. But life was so much better when you had someone.

Of course, I didn't *have* Chance.

But damn did I ever want him.

At least for tonight. Maybe more.

Probably more.

I'd been searching for Everly's music on a streaming service on my phone during the short drive home. Once I was in the kitchen, I set my phone on the counter and pushed Play while I helped myself to a glass of water. I hadn't heard this song, called "Clear-Hearted," before tonight.

When Everly had introduced it, she'd said the lyrics had flowed out of her in less than an hour one day and that they came from her heart and her life. The mellow song was about her future unfurling in a good way, about life feeling right at long last, as her path became clear and meaningful.

Knowing what little I did about her personally—that she was head over heels in love with her husband, Seth, and they were visibly expecting their first baby—it made perfect sense to me.

I felt the song in my soul. Not necessarily about Chance, because who knew where we would end up, but about my pregnancy and this town and the people I was getting to know. I was starting to feel like I might be right where I belonged.

As I set the glass down after drinking half of it, Chance came up beside me at the counter. The only light on was the one over the table, which we'd left on a dim setting while we were gone. When he peered down at me in the low light, extended his hand, and said, "May I have this dance?" my insides melted.

I smiled up at him and took his hand. Our bodies met as we wound our arms around each other and found the slow rhythm. As we swayed together, he trailed his hands below my waist, over my butt. He pulled me even closer, letting me feel his hardness at my core, telling me the drive home hadn't cooled him down either.

With hot need instantly pulsing through my body, I lifted my gaze to his. Our lips met at once, and it was as if the wind caught a spark and blew it into an inferno in a flash. As if both of us had been wanting this all night, thinking about it, imagining it throughout the concert and the drive home, and now that we were home, alone, we could finally get our hands and mouths on each other.

"God, Rowan," he said between frenetic kisses, his hands all over me.

"I know."

I kissed him with all the pent-up need that'd been building for weeks, grasping the back of his head, not about to let him get away from me.

Chance slipped his hands under my shirt and ran them

over my skin, kneading me, caressing me as if he couldn't get enough.

"I want you," he said as he angled us against the cabinets and pressed his body into me.

"Same," I managed as his fingers brushed across my oversensitive nipple. Even with the bra material between us, his touch made me want to climb him.

He pulled his head back from mine and made eye contact, both of us breathing hard. "Is this okay?" he asked. "I mean, with your pregnancy?"

"Yes." I cradled his handsome cheek in my palm.

"Thank fuck."

He brought his mouth to mine again, and we kissed like we were starving for each other, our tongues twisting and tangling, teeth hitting, breaths stuttering together.

"Where's Sam?" I finally thought to ask, pulling away enough to listen and ensure she wasn't in the basement.

"Exactly where she said she'd be. At Kinsley's. I checked on the way inside."

I was happy to hear that on multiple levels.

"We should take this upstairs though," he said, reading my thoughts. "Since she has a history of not staying put."

"Right. I think she's in a different place, so to speak, but it's better to be safe."

Chance took both my hands in his and wove our fingers together by our hips, our bodies still touching. "You're...okay with this?"

If we went up those stairs together, we'd be changing the rules.

I was more than okay with it.

I stretched up, kissed him, and whispered, "Let's go."

He tugged me behind him and flipped the light off as he hurried for the stairs, not that I needed tugging. I loved the feel of his hand though, his larger, stronger fingers surrounding mine.

At the top of the stairs, he didn't hesitate. He took a right and led me into his bedroom. Once he'd shut the door behind us, he turned on the lamp on his nightstand as I pulled my tunic-style shirt over my head.

"I've regretted not seeing you last time," he said as he came toward me.

"I don't quite look the same as I did on New Year's Eve." I touched my belly. He probably couldn't tell the difference, but I could, especially when I tried to wear jeans. I'd opted for leggings tonight because they stretched over my extra curves.

"You look beautiful." He busied himself unbuttoning his shirt, but his eyes didn't leave my body as I kicked off my boots and peeled my leggings down my legs.

I shoved my socks off with them, then stood in nothing but my lavender lace bra and underwear. They matched and were nearly new thanks to my boobs getting bigger and requiring me to go shopping.

"Gorgeous," Chance said, closing the space between us.

He'd unbuttoned his jeans and removed his shoes, looking delectable with his fit, solid upper body bared, a line of hair trailing down his muscled abdomen and disappearing beneath his jeans.

Instead of taking off the rest of his clothes, he ran his hands over me, down my back, over my butt, to my upper thighs, up again. He stepped back enough to peer at my belly and caressed it. Just a single reverent brush of his hand over my admittedly small, not-really-showing-yet belly. Before I could let the tenderness of that gesture sink in, he palmed my breast with one hand and reached behind me to unfasten my bra with the other. I shrugged it to the floor.

My nipples were so sensitive that just his breath fluttering over one of them made me gasp and arch closer to his mouth. When he closed his lips over the tip, I felt a tight, hollow pull at my core.

"Chance," I gasped out.

"Mm-hmm?"

"Get your clothes off."

"How about you get them off for me?"

He'd barely gotten the words out before I slid my hands down the inside back of his jeans and underwear, over his perfect butt, taking both layers of fabric down at once. He growled and moved to the edge of the bed, then lowered himself to the mattress, yanking his pants the rest of the way off.

As I stepped between his knees, he slid my panties down my legs, his gaze at the apex of my thighs making me burn lava-hot as I stepped out of them. He grasped my butt with both hands, kneading my cheeks as he roved his gaze upward and made eye contact. "If anything doesn't feel right," he said as I straddled him, my knees on either side of his hips, his dick teasing me, "we stop."

"The only thing that doesn't feel right is that you're not inside me."

"You better do something about that then," he said with a sexy smirk.

He palmed my breast and brought it to his mouth. The way he flicked his tongue over my nipple drew a gasp from me and intensified the hollow, needful ache between my legs.

"Condom?" I managed to ask.

He met my eyes with a grin. "So you don't get pregnant?" He swirled his tongue around the very tip of my nipple. "I'm clean."

"Me too," I said as I wrapped my hand around his shaft and lined him up with my entrance. In the next breath, I joined our bodies, impaling myself, letting out a slow moan at the delicious sensation.

Chance's head fell back, a look of ecstasy on his face that gave me the last bit of confidence I needed.

I ground my hips into him, watching his lust-heavy eyes, learning what he liked most, with the single goal of making him lose control. His hands were all over me, his talented fingers making it hard for me to keep my gaze locked on him. I'd never had a man look me in the eyes as we made love. The depth of the connection I felt with him was unlike anything I'd ever experienced.

I sought out his mouth, wanting to taste him again, craving the feel of his hungry lips locking with mine, devouring me.

When he angled his body up and thrust harder into me, palming my butt with both hands, I threw my head back at the exquisite feel of his onslaught. My attempts to make him lose control were backfiring. I couldn't think straight and stopped trying, merely holding on and riding him like a crazed, insatiable woman.

"Take what you need," he said in a sexy, growly command. "Come for me, Rowan."

I shifted my legs to cross them behind his back, our bodies moving as one to a frantic, escalating rhythm. He banded one arm around me, holding me tightly, and pinched and teased my nipple with his other hand.

My orgasm came on like a runaway truck out of nowhere, barreling over me, drawing sounds and words out of me that I had no control over. I didn't care. All I cared about was the sheer ecstasy that overtook me.

"Fuck, Rowan," he gritted out, arching higher, clinging tighter, thrusting harder a final time as he found his release.

With our bodies locked together, both of us momentarily wringing out every blissful second, it was as if there was a crack in the time continuum, and this moment was all that existed.

Several heartbeats later, our bodies went lax, and together we collapsed onto the bed, with me sprawling gracelessly on top of him. My heart pounded as I remembered how to breathe, and my body reluctantly eased back toward functioning.

I became aware of Chance's arms wrapped tightly around me, as if he wouldn't let me go. I melted into his body, breathed him in as my senses came online again.

"Are you doing okay?" he eventually whispered in my ear.

"Very okay," I answered drowsily.

"No pain or anything?"

I kissed his rough jaw as I realized he was worried about the pregnancy. "Everything's good. Pregnant people do that all the time."

"I know." He brushed my hair back. "Just making sure."

As my body came down from stupendously good sex, I shivered.

"Cold?" Chance asked.

"Starting to be."

He shifted and pulled the covers back, and I crawled under them.

"Be right back," he said, then kissed me and went to the master bathroom. As sated and boneless as I felt, I made a point of watching him walk away so I could admire his naked body.

I growled lazily and said, "Ten."

He paused at the door to the bathroom and turned back to me with a confused expression.

"That ass," I said, too boneless to point. "Ten."

He laughed as he closed the door between us.

I snuggled into the blankets, a dopey smile on my face, thinking it wasn't just his backside. The whole man was a solid ten in my book.

Chapter Twenty-Eight

Chance

As I crawled into my bed, I shut down on the faint stirring of uneasiness. Instead I focused on the naked woman snuggling into me.

"Welcome back," she whispered drowsily.

"Did you miss me?" I ran my hands over her warm, soft skin.

She took a couple of seconds to respond, as if she was about to fall asleep. "Tons. It's cold out there."

"Ah, so you just want me for my body heat," I teased. "I see how you are."

She ran a hand lazily up my chest, tucked her head into me, our legs tangling together. "Heat is nice," she mumbled. "But it's more because..." She went quiet, her breaths audible and even, and I thought she'd drifted off. "I love you, Chance."

Everything in me tensed. Rowan's breathing deepened. Her words had been a whisper, but I'd heard them clear as a bell.

My eyes popped wide-open, heart pounding. None of which she could discern even if she was partially awake. I didn't move. Waited for my freak-out to pass.

I realized I was holding my breath, then expelled it noiselessly.

Rowan wasn't conscious enough to notice her declaration had me crawling out of my skin.

I forced my eyes closed. Attempted to breathe evenly and calm my system.

I couldn't seem to rein in the panic, couldn't concentrate on my breaths because my brain had locked up.

Love? She couldn't love me. We weren't going there, couldn't go there. We'd agreed and for good reasons. Valid reasons.

Co-parenting was a partnership. We needed to keep it more like a business relationship than a messy, emotional one. That was the only way it would work for the long haul.

Sleeping together tonight was a serious mistake. I never, ever should've let it happen again. I'd fucked up. I'd turned off the logical part of my brain and gone with what my body wanted. My body and possibly my heart.

That thought had my blood going cold with pure, unadulterated fear. I shifted to my back abruptly, involuntarily. Anxiety pumped through me, turning off my brain again, sending me the message I was in trouble, pushing me to escape.

My chest felt compressed as my heartbeat raced, and I couldn't get a full breath. I broke out into a sweat. I had to get away before I lost my shit all the way.

I rolled to the edge of the mattress, unable to worry about whether I disturbed Rowan, and climbed out of the bed. Feeling as if the walls were closing in on me, I grabbed the sweats draped over my dresser and pulled them on as I hurried out of the room, down the stairs, and into my office.

Leaving the lights off, I sat heavily in the armchair, braced my elbows on my thighs, and ran my hands over my face, feeling the damp sheen of sweat on my forehead. I squeezed my eyes shut and begged my brain to snap the hell out of this.

————

Rowan

As I awakened, I took a moment to remember where I was.

Chance's room. Chance's bed.

My lips curved into a contented smile as I rolled over and reached for him. Not finding him, I extended my arm farther. The sheets on his side were cold, the blankets shoved back.

"Chance?" I said quietly.

Receiving no reply, I glanced toward the bathroom and could tell in the darkness that the door was open. He wasn't in the bathroom.

Wondering what time it was, sensing it was nowhere near morning, I tried to remember where my phone was. Likely on the counter in the kitchen.

Confused, I rolled out of bed and stood. The air was chilly on my naked body. I shivered as I felt around for something to put on. I came up with Chance's button-down shirt and snuggled into it gratefully. Then I frowned, wondering where the heck he could be.

Maybe Sam had come home after all?

The other three doors on the second level were all open, telling me no one was in them.

Note to self: If you're trying to pull off a secret tryst in Chance's bedroom, at least make it look like you're in your room by closing the door.

With a private, lustful smile, I imagined sneaking to his room frequently. Now that we'd had another taste, I didn't see us staying away from each other.

I stood at the top of the stairs and listened. The house was silent.

My smile faded, and alarm crept in with every breath as I went down the carpeted stairs without making a noise.

I took a right at the bottom, glancing into the formal living room as I passed, able to see by the light filtering in through the blinds it was empty.

On to the kitchen. The clock on the stove blared out that it was 3:07 a.m., a time that made no sense for anything other than being in bed.

My concern inched up as I went into the dark family room to make sure Chance wasn't in there. I peeked out the door to the patio. It was deserted as usual.

It had to be that Sam was home, maybe upset, and he was in the basement with her, comforting her. I went back to the kitchen and opened the door to the basement. It was dark and silent, telling me my conclusion was wrong.

As I closed the basement door, I realized I hadn't checked Chance's office. It had two doors, one from the kitchen and one at the foot of the stairs. The kitchen one was closed, so I went around the central staircase again and found the other door open.

When I stepped inside, I saw him sitting shirtless in his armchair, legs stretched out on the ottoman. His elbow was braced on one of the arms, hand supporting his head. Thinking he was asleep, I gave myself a few seconds to appreciate the sight of him in the dim light from outside, shadows playing over his half-naked body.

"Hey," I said quietly, not wanting to startle him.

I watched his chest rise slowly with a deep breath. Then his head came up as he finally looked at me. I realized he hadn't been asleep. Concern spiked through me again.

"What's going on?" I asked, walking closer.

I found a corner of the ottoman to perch on in front of him.

He dropped his legs to the floor, leaned forward, elbows on knees. My relief at finding him had disappeared as an alarm went off in my head telling me very clearly he was not okay, and it likely had to do with us.

"Talk to me, Chance," I said, not bothering to keep my voice hushed. "Why are you down here?"

He stood, as if he didn't want to be so close to me. I tried to let that roll off, but I was getting the distinct impression he'd slammed a metaphorical door shut with me on the outside.

"I'm sorry, Rowan. Tonight..." He shook his head as he paced. "That never should've happened. I shouldn't have let it. I told myself we're both adults, and it's fine for us to find pleasure in each other, but it's not going to work."

My heart pounded as I realized speaking my feelings before I'd dozed off must have spooked him. "I freaked you out with the L-word."

"We can't do that."

"Do that? Fall in love?"

"Right. We had an agreement."

"We did, but we changed it. It seemed like both of us went into that willingly."

"I let myself believe we could handle it, but there's too much between us. Our priority has to be the baby."

"I agree."

"We can't be lovers. We can't fall in love. Love would ruin everything."

That was so absurd I had to hold in a disbelieving laugh. He clearly believed that. "Tell me why."

He dropped into his desk chair. "We have to focus on the baby," he said again.

"And you don't think we can do that if we love each other?"

"Love would take away our chance of making it through the next two decades on good terms."

"I don't understand, Chance. This is new"—I gestured between us—"and I'm not trying to rush us or make us something we're not yet, but how can you say feelings between us wouldn't be beneficial for our child? It doesn't make sense."

He popped up off the chair and paced again, his agitation growing. At the doorway, he reached up, grabbed the doorjamb, and held on, facing away from me. Silence stretched out, my heart racing as I waited, wondered what he could possibly say that would make sense.

Finally he let go of the doorjamb, turned halfway, leaned his back against the frame, and crossed his arms. "The problem is me, Rowan. Look at my track record. Every single relationship that should be strong is a mess. My daughter. My parents. My brother. Erin. I'm the weak link. I've tried my whole life to be what my loved ones need, and I've fallen short. Every. Last. Time."

"What?" I nearly shrieked. "You can't really think that." His nonresponse told me he did.

I let that sink in, tried to comprehend it. In my opinion, it was crazy, but I was starting to see he actually believed there was something wrong with him.

I stood from the ottoman. "Your daughter is a *teenager*, Chance. Teenagers are impossible."

"Yet you got along with her within five minutes of meeting her. Now she talks to you ten times more than she talks to me. I'm glad she has you," he added quickly. "Damn glad she has you because I can't fucking seem to do anything right when it comes to helping her."

"That's not true. She knows you love her. I think she feels awkward talking to you because you're her dad."

"I can't change that. I don't know what do to improve our relationship, and that's what I'm fucking talking about. I suck at relationships. Every kind."

"You do not," I said with conviction. His parents had done a job on him. It was now becoming clear how much their indifference, if that's what it was, had burrowed deep into him and affected him. "I've never met your parents, but from what I've heard, they're self-centered, self-important people too blind to see what a wonderful person their son is. And your wife..." I approached him and touched his forearm, still crossed with the other one as if to shut me out. "Chance, your wife was an addict. That had nothing to do with you."

"What if it did?"

"It didn't."

"You don't know that."

"What I know is you," I said. "I know what kind of man you are, and I know she was a lucky woman to have you."

"She didn't seem to think so." He pushed himself off the doorframe with a loud sigh. "I'm sorry. Forget about Erin. I know addiction was a factor. We've gotten off track."

"It seems like we're right on track."

"The point is I'm messed up," he said quietly, earnestly.

"I don't have a good history with long-term relationships, and I don't believe it would be smart for us to get closer. We agreed on our goal, Rowan, and that's raising our child. I don't want anything to endanger our ability to do that. It's better if we make it more of a businesslike relationship."

Businesslike? I was admittedly new to raising kids, but I was pretty damn sure it was anything but businesslike.

"We've basically been in a relationship for weeks. Everything but sleeping together. We spend most of our waking ours together, talk every day, eat together, work together... We've been *doing* a relationship, Chance."

"I can't knowingly continue that. Not with the stakes."

I stared at him across the dark room. "So that's it? You quit? Never mind what we started or how we feel?"

"It's the smart thing to do."

"Fuck smart, Chance. I can't just unfeel things. I meant what I said. I love you."

"I'm sorry, Rowan." He said it with so much finality I wanted to slap some sense into him.

I wasn't a violent person, had never hit anyone in my life, but if ever there was a moment that called for it..."You don't even want to try?" I asked in disbelief.

He shook his head.

"The baby won't be born for six months," I said. "That's a lot of time for a trial run."

"And when it doesn't work out, we still have a birth and a kid's entire life to navigate."

When it didn't work out? I stared at him with my mouth gaping open. This side of him was...unexpected to say the least. "What if it *did* work out, Chance?"

He uncrossed his arms, shook his head. "Not going to go there."

All I could do was stare at him as I tried to process his complete, utter cowardice. I'd known he was reluctant to get involved, but I had way underestimated his fear.

"You won't even consider trying?" I finally managed. "You won't let things develop slowly, naturally, and see what happens?"

He wouldn't look at me now. I'd never, ever seen even a hint of this side of Chance.

I felt sick to my stomach, sheer, utter disappointment bubbling up like acid. And heartbreak? My chest throbbed with an ache that made it difficult to breathe. I felt as if my heart was literally cracking into pieces.

The plummet from blissful euphoria two hours ago to this... I hadn't seen it coming. Not even a hint. This was a T-bone blindside accident on the driver's side, crushing me on impact.

"You should go to bed, Rowan," he said, still not looking at me. "Try to get some sleep. I'm not changing my mind."

I narrowed my eyes and summoned the energy to spit out at him, "I have experience with hopeless situations. There was no hope for my Gram, but she had no choice in the matter. It's the most grim, awful way to exist. But you... You're *choosing* to live without hope. That's the most tragic, pathetic, disappointing thing I've ever heard of." My voice, low with conviction and emotion, cracked a little, but I wasn't done yet. "I can't fix that for you, Chance. Only you can. Sadly you're not the only one losing out because of your cowardice."

He squeezed his eyes closed, the first sign I'd seen that he might have any regrets or second thoughts. I waited to see if he'd change his mind. Gave him the chance to backpedal. All he did was drop into his desk chair and swivel away from me.

I guess I had my final answer.

"I'll find another place to live," I said quietly, then turned and left him there alone. The way he wanted to be for the rest of his life.

Chapter Twenty-Nine

Rowan

On Sunday I tried my best to act like it was just another day. Tried to pretend my heart didn't feel like it'd been shoved through a meat grinder.

I was in the back seat of Presley's car, Chloe was riding shotgun, and we were finally going to see the lakefront house Presley had bought. Though my eyes were gritty with fatigue, I welcomed the excuse to get out of Chance's house for a couple of hours. A couple *more* hours, as I'd also taken Sam to another knitting session at Fat Cat.

After leaving Chance's office in the wee hours of the morning, I'd closed myself in my room the way I should've done from the start. I hadn't even tried to sleep, knowing it would elude me. Instead I'd dived back into the search for a place to live.

I'd discovered nothing had really changed. There were still very few listings in Dragonfly Lake. The only one I'd found in my budget was in the town of Runner, about fifteen miles away. I'd never been there and didn't love the idea of starting over in yet another place, even though I'd still be working at the brewery.

I was desperate to live somewhere else though and had even searched for rentals in Nashville. The problem was rent was higher in a large city, and when you added the cost of commuting an hour each way, it didn't make sense. I'd be better off finding a job in Nashville, but that wasn't what I wanted at all.

I apparently wasn't going to get what I wanted, so I needed to find my plan B and get started on it.

I'd get back to searching tonight.

"Here we are," Presley said as she turned into a driveway on the lake side of Honeysuckle Road.

"Two doors down from Max Dawson," Chloe said.

That Presley could buy a house in the same neighborhood as a former NFL player—with cash—said a lot.

She pulled up in front of a three-car garage that was connected to a cottage-style white-with-gray-stonework home.

"Nice," Chloe said.

"It looks beautiful from here," I agreed.

"The exterior is in good shape, thank God," Presley said as she opened her door. "The inside, well, you'll see."

The three of us went in the front door, where we could see through a large room with tall windows to the lake beyond.

"That view is amazing," Chloe said.

"I can't wait to see it in the summer." Presley closed the door and gestured us forward.

The three of us wandered around the empty three-thousand-square-foot house, talking as we went.

"I forgot to tell you guys, Bronte Henry was born at

nine forty-seven this morning," Chloe said, her voice animated, as we started with the master bedroom. "Eight pounds, two ounces."

"Bronte. Adorable name," Presley said.

"Not a small baby, from what I've read," I said. "Ava and Bronte are doing well? And of course Cash?"

"Everyone's healthy and happy," Chloe said. "I cannot wait to meet her. This view? A bed right here? I don't think I'd ever get out."

"I call bullshit. You'd never be able to *not* work," Presley said, laughing. "I have to admit the idea of a view from my bed was part of what made me jump at this house. And the outdoor space is incredible."

After showing us the master bath, which was large and functional but outdated by her standards, she led us to the living area, explaining her ideas for gutting it, the dining room, and the kitchen to open it all up and update it. "The sunroom was another selling point," she said as we spun around to admire the windowed breakfast area off the kitchen.

As we toured the upstairs, which had two bedroom suites, an unfinished storage room, and a loft, Presley told us the latest on her insufferable boss in between pointing out features she either wanted redone or that she loved.

"This has so much potential," Chloe said. "I just have one question."

"Oh, this should be good," Presley quipped as she led us back down to the main floor.

"What in the world are you going to do with all this space? Three thousand square feet for one person? You could fit three of my house in here."

"I told you I might rent it out," Presley said, unconcerned. "Or live here. Who knows. It's good to have options."

I would do just about anything for a few options right now. I kept the thought to myself, as I hadn't told the girls what had happened between Chance and me. I didn't want to think about it.

Once we stood out on the spacious deck, gazing at the lake, with me in the middle of the other two, however, Chloe leaned into me with her shoulder. "I've waited as long as I could to bring it up. You and Chance seemed *close* last night at the Fly. Yeah?"

"Ooh, I called it," Presley said from my other side. "Living with the father of your baby, when he looks like that and you're still attracted?" She laughed. "A girl wouldn't stand a chance."

I inhaled deeply, the ache in my chest intensifying when I let the air back out.

"That didn't sound like a girl-in-love sigh though," Presley said, eyeing me from the side.

Chloe turned and leaned her backside against the railing, scrutinizing me. I met her gaze, and she could apparently read beneath the surface because she said, "Oh, no. What happened?"

I pressed my lips together, as if I could hold in the feelings I'd been trying to stave off all day. It didn't work.

Tears rolled down my cheeks before I could get a word out. Presley put an arm around me and pulled me into her side. Chloe held on to my hand.

I opened my mouth to start the story I needed to get out. "We—" My voice cracked. "I..."

Presley reached up to wipe her own eyes even though I hadn't gotten a single sentence out yet.

"I need to find a place to live," I finally said on a wail.

Before I knew what was happening, my two friends pulled me into a group hug, which unleashed the sobs I'd been avoiding since walking away from Chance. I'd cried so much in the past six months. I was so, so tired of feeling like I'd been filleted, exposed, bleeding out in the form of saltwater.

"Let it out, babe," Presley cooed.

As if I had any choice. My heartbreak gushed out of me in an ugly cry.

These girls, these beautiful friends of mine, just held me, encouraged me to purge the sadness, let me know I wasn't alone.

Eventually the sobs slowed, and I was able to get out, "S-s-s-sorry," between hiccups. "I'm a mess."

"Between life, stupid boys, and pregnancy hormones, you are entitled to be as big of a mess as you need to be," Chloe said.

"H-how do you kn-now the boy was stupid?" I stuttered out.

"Because he's a boy," Presley answered without hesitation.

Laughter bubbled out even as I cried, which made all of us laugh harder, still holding on to each other.

When I could finally speak coherently, I straightened, wove one arm with Presley's and one with Chloe's, and stepped to the railing, taking them with me, keeping them on each side of me.

I let the story pour out, from the magic of last night's concert to the slow dance in the kitchen to what I thought was a magical connection in Chance's bed. My admission of love, which turned out to be the nail in the coffin of our blink-and-you'll-miss it relationship. Chance's refusal to see where it might've gone.

"Blazes of hell, girlfriend." Presley again put her arm around me and rested her head on my upper arm. "That's the last twenty-four hours?"

"More like twelve," I said.

"And he thinks, what, you're just gonna change diapers and feed the baby together like nothing ever happened?" Presley continued.

"I don't know." I couldn't begin to think about what that would be like. "I know it was fast, but I love that stupid man," I said, sniffling.

"You went quiet, Chlo," Presley said. "You could fire him, couldn't you?"

Presley and I laughed, but I noticed Chloe didn't.

"I'm so surprised by him," Chloe said pensively, gripping the railing. "I know Chance. Like, I know him well. There's gotta be some serious fear going on there, because it's just not like him to be cold and unyielding."

I knew what she meant, and of course I agreed he was scared. It didn't make me feel any better.

"Screw that," Presley said emphatically. "We all have fears, but sometimes you've gotta step up and find a way around it. If he thinks *this* is going to be better for a kid, he's dumber than dumb."

"Ah, my eloquent friend," Chloe said. "But I agree."

"So you're going to move out?" Presley asked.

"As soon as I can find a place." I'd even considered moving back into the Honeysuckle Inn.

"I'd offer to let you stay with us, but all we've got is a couch," Chloe said.

"You're sweet." I didn't mention it would be awkward to live with both my bosses. Chloe was becoming a friend first and foremost, but Holden was the guy in charge of everything.

"You know what?" Presley said, casual as could be. "I have an extra house you could borrow."

Chloe and I both angled a look at her.

"You do have an extra house," Chloe said slowly. "It's... kind of empty but..."

Presley scoffed. "We could move the furniture from the spare bedroom in my condo tonight."

"We could pick up a second-hand couch and a TV," Chloe added.

"I don't need a TV," I said, "but I can't move into your house before you do."

"Of course you can." Presley became animated. "I don't even know if or when I'm moving in. It's just sitting here until I can hire a contractor. You can stay in one of the upstairs bedrooms for as long as you need. I mean, it might suck that ninety percent of the house is empty, but we can fix that gradually. The main thing is you could get out right away. No more awkward nights locking yourself in your bedroom in that stupidhead's house."

"Yes," Chloe said. "He's my employee and good friend, but he's being a stupidhead, and you need a refuge."

I thought about this big, empty house that was more than I'd probably ever have for myself. It would be a little odd to stay here, but... I shuddered as I imagined waking up in Chance's house every morning, running into him in the hallway in my pajamas, making life uncomfortable for poor Sam. Presley's offer was hard to resist.

"Let's do it," Presley said. "If we leave now and drive straight to my condo, we can load up enough for tonight and get the rest tomorrow."

"You think we can fit the bed into my SUV?" Chloe asked.

"Good thing you got the biggest model," Presley teased.

"Kind of like you got the biggest model of house," Chloe shot back.

I stood between them, half listening to their banter while I considered my options. Because suddenly I did have an option.

My heart felt heavy with sadness at the thought of moving out and distancing myself from Chance. I'd apparently been harboring more hope for a happily-ever-after between us than I'd ever realized. This was me throwing my hands up and admitting that was a pipe dream. As hard as that was, though, I needed to do it. The only way to move forward, start healing from this latest loss, and prepare for being a mom was to make a clean break. I'd still have to work with him, but it was easier to keep boundaries at work than in the place I called home.

"You went quiet, Rowan," Presley said. She wove our arms together again. "Are you on board, hon?"

I turned my mind to practical matters for now. "I'll pay you rent and move out as soon as I can find a place for my baby and me."

"No rent, and we'll help you search, but there's no rush other than your due date," Presley said. "And that's only because I know you want to settle in your own place. I'd never kick you out."

"I'm not living here for free."

"I paid cash," Presley reminded us matter-of-factly. "I don't have a mortgage. I'm not charging you rent."

"What if she paid for utilities?" Chloe said.

"Absolutely," I said.

"Perfect," Presley agreed.

So it was settled.

Presley and Chloe would make the Nashville run for

furniture while I packed all my belongings at Chance's and tried to figure out what to say to Sam.

The Chance romance chapter had turned out to be a very short, heartbreaking one, but now it was time for the next one. I'd be okay eventually. I'd already made it through a lot.

I reminded myself I'd learned strength from my beloved Gram. Strength and love. My baby would feel that love every day of their life and never doubt they were adored and cherished.

Sadly for him—and me—Chance would miss out on my love, but he'd made his choice.

Chapter Thirty

Chance

I drove into my garage after seven Tuesday evening and felt a pang at the empty bay next to mine. After killing the engine, I sat there in the dark, wondering how the hell I'd gotten so used to Rowan's presence in so little time.

When she'd packed up everything and left Sunday evening, I'd been stunned at both her haste to get out and that she'd found a place to go so quickly. I still didn't know where she was staying and refused to ask, but it was killing me not to know. Killing me more not to have her in my home.

Though we'd both been at work yesterday and today, Chloe had Rowan working closely with her on a project. Was it intentional to keep her from having to talk to me? I had no way of knowing and pretended it didn't matter.

Thinking about our middle-of-the-night conversation made me sick to my stomach. I'd been a complete asshole. The panic attack I'd had before it didn't excuse anything.

The expression on her face in that instant when she'd accepted I wouldn't change my mind—of hurt, disbelief, and disappointment—was seared into my brain. I hated myself for making her feel that way, especially knowing how much grief and sadness she'd been through so recently with her grandmother.

And fuck was I sick of feeling like this, but I didn't know a way around it.

I got out of my SUV and made my way inside, dreading another quiet night alone. When I entered the house, the first thing I noticed was the smell of food cooking, maybe Italian. I hurried into the kitchen, wondering if Rowan was back.

"Hi, Dad."

Of course Rowan wasn't back. Why the hell would she come back here? I'd made sure of that.

"Sam." I hoped that half-second of disappointment that she wasn't Rowan didn't show.

What kind of dad did that make me? Of course I was happy to see my daughter, particularly because she seemed warm instead of sullen.

"What's going on?" I asked, confused.

My daughter took a steaming, bubbling casserole dish that smelled like heaven out of the oven. "I made lasagna. Rowan gave me her Gram's recipe."

I looked from her to the pan and back. "You made lasagna? From scratch?"

Sam used to help me cook when she was younger, but I couldn't remember the last time she'd willingly made a meal for anyone other than herself.

"What's the occasion?" I asked, perplexed.

"Could you get us some plates? You got home just in time."

Still trying to make sense of this welcome surprise, I grabbed plates, forks, and napkins and put them on the table. Sam carried the pan to the table with two oven mitts and set it on a trivet. She went back to the kitchen, picked up a slotted spatula, returned to the table, and sat down.

I stood behind my place, probably with my jaw gaping.

"Do you want to eat?" she asked, snapping me out of my stupor.

I sat down. "Lasagna's a lot of work. Doesn't it take a couple of hours?"

"I started around five. I was worried it wouldn't be ready when you got home, but then you worked late." She cut generous squares of pasta and gestured to me to move my plate closer to the pan. When I did, she served me, her smile seeming unsure.

"I was finishing the social media calendar," I said.

The one that didn't need to be done for another three weeks, but I didn't admit that. Sam might get the impression I was avoiding coming home, which, of course I was, but it had nothing to do with her. Normally she spent all her time in her basement hideaway, popping up for fifteen minutes tops when dinner was ready. Had I known my daughter had surfaced and was preparing dinner, I wouldn't have worked so late. It was Rowan's absence I'd been hiding from.

"It smells amazing," I told her. "What made you decide to go to all this effort?"

She served herself, sat back down, and scooped a bite on her fork. "What happened between you and Rowan?"

I'd been blowing on my food to cool it, but I stopped. "What do you mean?"

"Come on, Dad. I'm fourteen. Stop treating me like I'm four."

Did I treat her like she was four? Hell, I didn't mean to.

Maybe I did? She was still my little girl. Would always be my little girl.

"Rowan always planned to find her own place," I said. The truth. Well, at least it'd started out that way.

"She didn't move to her own place."

So Sam had been in touch with Rowan at some point. I was heartened to learn that, but at the same time, it hit hard that I was the outsider now.

It was on the tip of my tongue to ask my daughter where Rowan had moved. I bit down on it.

When Sam finished a mouthful of food, she scowled. "I'm not stupid. You spent almost every evening with her since she moved in. It was super obvious you two were involved. She moved out suddenly, and you've been sad ever since."

Well, then. My daughter picked up on a hell of a lot more from the basement than I'd ever guessed. Apparently I was the stupid one.

"I'm sorry if I treat you like a little kid," I said, meaning it. "I don't have any experience being a dad of a teenage girl. I didn't understand teenage girls when I was a teenager myself, and it hasn't gotten any easier." I tried to make the comment light, but it fell flat.

"What did you do to make her mad?"

"Your age aside, my relationship with Rowan is private, Sam."

"This is why we aren't close, Dad. We can't talk about anything except my stupid grades and whether I've spoken to Lacey. I haven't, by the way, and I'm not going to. She's mean and only cares about herself."

"I don't know Lacey well, but I think you're right."

"I don't care about her anyway."

We both stuck another bite of lasagna in our mouths. I

welcomed the minibreak so I could try to figure out how to navigate this situation.

"You like Rowan, don't you?" I asked.

Sam nodded, then swallowed. "I miss her." She tilted her head and studied me. "You love her, don't you?"

I was about to scoop up another bite, but my fork froze. My mouth went dry, and a knot tightened in my gut. "What makes you say that?"

"I can just tell by the way you are around her. Like, you're lighter somehow. Definitely happier."

This was not a comfortable topic, but I'd just been accused of treating her like a child. What I really wanted to do was divert, change the subject. She might be right that I'd been treating her like a child. I suspected she'd see right through me if I refused to answer. As vulnerable as it made me feel, I decided to try being open.

I tapped my fork on my plate as I considered my response. "I care about Rowan," I finally said. "Obviously I find her attractive or we wouldn't be in this situation."

"Please don't tell me gross details," she pleaded, making me grin briefly.

"There's a lot to like about Rowan. She's smart, funny, caring, compassionate..." I stopped myself from listing more, even as several other of her good traits came to mind. "She's carrying my child, and that connects us in a lifelong way. But love?" I set my fork on the table, my mind going eight hundred miles per hour. I shook my head, as if I could stave my feelings off, even as the very real fear seeped in that it was too late. "I don't know. I've avoided falling in love since your mom."

"I've seen you and Rowan together a lot," Sam said. "I've seen how you are with her. How often you smile. The way you look at her. The way you listen to everything she says and consider it. How you always look out for her, make sure she's taken care of." She nodded matter-of-factly. "And did I mention the way you look at her?"

"You did."

"You get this certain look in your eyes. And I'm pretty sure Rowan feels the same about you."

I gave her a noncommittal grunt. I wasn't going to share that Rowan had said she loved me. I already felt itchy and uncomfortable.

Sam frowned, looking thoughtfully at her nearly empty plate. "Maybe you're just scared."

My brows shot up as my eyes popped wide-open. I turned that over in my mind. It didn't take long for it to resonate, as much as I didn't want to admit it. But hell yes, I was scared to love someone. I felt that in my bones.

Shit. Called out by my fourteen-year-old daughter.

My instinct was to deny it. Who wanted to look weak to their kid?

I met Sam's gaze. Instead of judgment or disgust, I saw empathy and understanding in her eyes.

With an uneasy chuckle, I said, "Yeah. Maybe I'm just scared."

"Rowan isn't Mom, Dad."

My daughter was one hundred percent right. Logically I knew that. Rowan didn't have an addiction that would take her away from me.

"This isn't the same," Sam continued. "At all."

"Yeah." I took in a deep breath, let that truth sink in, breathed out the fear.

Rowan was different from Erin.

I was different from the man I'd been fifteen years ago.

"You always used to tell me it's okay to be afraid as long as you don't let it keep you from living your life," Sam said.

Damn if I hadn't. I steepled my hands in front of me while I let it sink in that my daughter had just thrown my words back at me. You never knew if your kid actually heard anything you said. The bitch of it was she was right, and I knew it.

I'd been protecting myself from the truth for two days. Hell, maybe two months.

I loved Rowan.

It'd taken my daughter pointing it out, insisting on it, for me to acknowledge it.

"When did you get so smart?" I asked her.

"I was born this way," she said with a sassy smirk.

All other things aside, that bit of attitude and confidence did my dad heart proud. She'd seemed to have lost her confidence back when she was trying to fit in with Lacey and friends.

"So you're admitting it?" she asked.

"Admitting what?"

"You love Rowan."

I sucked in another slow breath, breaking out in a sweat. My heart pounded so hard I could feel it in my temples.

I pictured Rowan's pretty eyes when they were full of flirtation and life and laser focused on me. Remembered the way she looked when she was learning something new, determined to conquer it. Recalled the depths of love in her expression when she talked about her grandmother. Thought about how she'd been sensitive to Sam's needs from the first day she'd met her.

I liked her, respected her, wanted to protect her with every cell in my body from anything and everything that could hurt her. Longed to wake up next to her each morning and end every evening with her in my arms. To comfort her and be comforted by her through life's challenges. To revel in every milestone and success together—ours, Sam's, our baby's, our family's.

I wanted all of that. With Rowan.

"Yes," I finally said, sitting up straighter, feeling lighter as soon as I'd said it. More alive. "I love Rowan. I'm not sure what to do about that."

"Tell her," she said with the naivete of a fourteen-year-old.

"I'm pretty sure she doesn't want to hear it."

"Were you a jerk to her?"

I raised my brows.

"You were," she said.

I nodded.

"You'll need to grovel then."

Yeah. I'd need to grovel my damn heart out to even get Rowan to listen to me.

Sam stood and gathered both our plates, then carried them to the counter. I grabbed the lasagna pan and followed, my mind churning over how on earth I could convince Rowan to give me another chance.

Once I set the pan down, I held my arms out to my daughter for a hug, holding my breath, afraid she'd reject it.

She stepped into my arms and wrapped hers around me. "If you want, I can help you come up with a grand gesture she won't be able to refuse," she said.

I closed my eyes and wondered when my little girl had learned about grand gestures and grovels. "I'd love that, Sammy."

I squeezed her tight, grateful for this girl who'd gone out of her way tonight, offering an olive branch in the form of pasta and encouragement.

For the first time in days, I felt a faint pulse of hope.

Chapter Thirty-One

Rowan

Something jolted me out of a light slumber. I lifted my head from the pillow and tried to get my bearings.

I was in my bedroom at Presley's, which she'd insisted on making cozy and comfortable, bordering on luxurious. The bed from her condo's guest room had a soft, feminine, upholstered headboard, a fluffy white comforter, and cloud-like sheets. Even though I'd said I didn't need a TV, she'd brought one over, saying I might want it for noise since the rest of the house was so empty.

She'd been right. The TV was on now, still playing *Gilmore Girls* episodes. I'd seen them all before, but Sam and I had discussed the show a week ago, which made me want to rewatch.

I looked at the TV, trying to figure out whether something on the show had woken me up. Just then, a light ping came from the large, four-panel window that looked out over the lake, sounding like tiny hail or sleet. Except the weather had been springlike and clear today.

A glance at my phone told me it was a few minutes after eight p.m. Dark outside. When another ping came, my heart sped up in alarm, and I came fully awake. Had I locked the doors downstairs? I only used one, and I was pretty militant about checking it.

The lights in my room were off, the only illumination the flickering of the television. I felt around for the remote, found it buried in the covers, and clicked off the TV, leaving me in the dark.

The ping came again. I crawled out of bed on the side away from the windows, my hand cradling my small belly automatically. Picking up my phone, I went to the opposite end of the window from where the pings were sounding and crept up to the closed blinds. My heart was in my throat, my finger perched over my phone's keypad, ready to dial 911.

The next ping sounded, again on the opposite end, which was a good eight feet away from me, giving me courage to pry the blinds open just enough to peek outside.

I nearly screamed at the sight of a man sitting a few feet away on top of the pergola. The moon was bright, enabling me to see that the guy held something over his head.

The second I recognized the boom box, I realized it was Chance, and I wilted in relief. Dropping my hand from the blinds, I pressed it to my chest to ease my frantic heart.

Once the message that there wasn't a killer outside my window registered, I stepped back to the blinds, surreptitiously peeking out again, confused and concerned.

Had he lost his damn mind? What would ever possess someone to climb to the top of a pergola that had to be a good fourteen feet off the ground? How had he gotten up there? Did he have a death wish?

As I watched, he pulled something out of his pocket and winged it at the window again, apparently still trying to get my attention.

All I could think was, what the actual hell was going through his head?

Frowning, I flipped the blinds open abruptly, my eyes locked on him. I went to the end he'd been hitting, raised the blinds completely, and cranked the window open.

"What in the world are you doing?" I exclaimed.

That's when I heard it. Music. Coming from the boom box he raised higher over his head now that he saw me. It only took a few notes for me to recognize the song—"In Your Eyes," the one we'd danced to that very first time on New Year's Eve.

"Oh," I said quietly, softening in spite of myself.

Chance continued to sit there, watching me as the music played. Once the shock and the subsequent emotional punch dissipated, I crossed my arms and leaned against the window frame, shivering in the chilly air, waiting him out. Because *what the hell?*

Still holding the radio up, he stood, wobbling slightly as he found his footing on the widely spaced two-by-fours that made up the pergola roof.

"What are you doing, you idiot?" I hissed, visions of him falling to his death plaguing me.

Chance made it all the way to the windows without dying, then lowered the boom box, the music still playing. The volume was low, so at least he wouldn't wake the neighbors.

"Seriously, what are you doing?" I asked, still coming down from that moment when he'd flirted with falling.

"I need to talk to you, Rowan."

I held up my phone, still with the keypad at the ready. "Have you heard of texting?"

"It's an in-person topic."

"Okay, so maybe knock on the door? You could break your neck up there."

"I was trying to make a point," he said quietly.

Something about his tone had me stepping back from my panic and taking in his gesture as a whole.

He was serenading me. Playing the first song we'd danced to. Enacting a scene from a movie. Standing out in the cool night on top of a pergola roof, for the love of God.

The question was why? He was the one who'd put an end to *us*. Was he afraid he'd lose access to our baby? I wouldn't ever do that without a damn good reason. Surely he knew me well enough to know that.

Had he changed his mind about us?

I shut down on the hope that single thought sprouted.

"So can we talk?" he asked, his brows rising.

I studied his handsome, earnest face, trying to read his intent. His expression gave away nothing.

Obviously I wasn't going to send him away without finding out what he wanted. I could tell him I'd meet him at the deck door, but the thought of him moving another foot on that pergola roof sent a shudder through me.

Shining the dim light of my phone on the window screen, I located a release toward the top. I reached up, slid the release over, and maneuvered the screen off the window. "Get in here," I told him.

Chance was in my second-floor bedroom in an instant, standing close enough I could smell his familiar scent. Maybe it would've been wiser to send him to the deck door after all. I wouldn't fall under his spell nearly as fast if we were six feet apart in the kitchen instead of a foot apart in my bedroom.

He set the radio on the floor, along the wall, the music continuing to play at a background level.

I stepped around him and slid the screen back into place, then cranked the window shut. Before I turned to face him, I collected myself, donned an indifferent expression, and tried to remember the impenetrable look on his face four nights ago when he'd figuratively pushed me away.

"Rowan," he said behind me.

I closed my eyes and tried not to be drawn in by the familiar, comforting timbre of his voice. The last four days had been hell as I'd tried to accept that I'd misjudged him, ending up with my heart taking the damage, plunging me deeper into a well of grief at yet another loss. I couldn't be sucked back into his orbit just at the sound of his voice saying my name, like a desperate puppy wanting to be loved.

He grasped my hand and tugged me gently away from the window. "Will you sit and hear me out?"

Sitting did sound divine. He gestured to the edge of the bed. I sat on it, keeping my legs on the floor because I wasn't about to get comfortable or let my guard down. Not when just being this close to him and my bed had spicy thoughts running through my mind.

Chance lowered himself to the mattress next to me. He pulled one of his legs up to pivot and face me from the side. "Will you look at me?"

I heard a hint of vulnerability in his question, so I mirrored his position and faced him in the moonlit room.

"Rowan, I'm sorry. I screwed up utterly and completely the other night."

I met his gaze. His eyes shone with regret and humility

as he took my hand in his and settled our entwined hands on his knee.

"You were right," he said. "When you told me you loved me, I freaked out. Those three words sent me into what I now know was an anxiety attack." He averted his gaze and swallowed hard before making eye contact again. "That's no excuse. I just want you to know that's how much the idea of a real, feelings-involved relationship scared me."

Any irritation and disappointment I might've been feeling slipped away. My heart went out to him. "I get it, Chance. Caring about someone is scary. The idea of possibly losing someone is horrible. The absolute worst, no matter how you lose them..."

"I know. I know that's a fresh wound for you with your Gram." He squeezed his eyes closed momentarily. "And I pushed you away when you were still recovering from her loss... Fuck, Rowan, I'm so sorry."

It wasn't okay; I still wasn't okay, but I nodded to let him know I could forgive him.

"My daughter called me on my bullshit," he said.

"Sam? What did she say?"

He let out a humorless chuckle. "She called me out for letting fear prevent me from living the life I want."

"That can happen."

"She got that from me." He shook his head. "I can't describe to you how it feels to have your teenage daughter come back at you with your own words. Particularly when she's right, because she was. I was letting fear hold me back from what I wanted. *Want*. You. A family. A real family. Love." He moved closer to me, our knees butting against each other. When he sought out my gaze again, the look in his eyes was fervent, impassioned, determined. "I love you, Rowan."

I stared at him, afraid to breathe. Afraid he'd realize what he'd said and take it back.

"I think I was halfway in love with you before the end of New Year's Eve," he continued. "There was a pull between us even then like nothing I've ever felt. I couldn't let myself go there though because…"

"Scared," I whispered.

"Scared," he repeated. "But I'm tired of letting fear win. Am I still scared? Hell yes. But I'm doing this anyway. I love you, Rowan Andrews."

Before I could say anything back, he slid off the edge of the bed to the floor. He got down on one knee, dug something out of his pocket, then held up a small velvet box.

I caught my breath, my heart thundering in a different way.

His eyes skipped up to meet mine as he opened the box and took out a stunning, sparkling ring. Holding it with one hand, he took my hand in his other. I could feel him shaking —or maybe that was me.

I pressed my lips together, trying to keep my emotions in so I wouldn't miss a second. To make sure I wasn't misunderstanding this, wasn't dreaming it up.

"I want to be a real family with you. Partners in every way. Parents of Sam and Bean there, co-chefs of our kitchen, dance partners for life. Will you marry me, Rowan?"

"Oh, my God." I looked into his beautiful, love-filled eyes, seeing the truth there. He'd decided to move forward, to leave his fear in the dust. "I love you, Chance. I can't wait to spend the rest of my life with you. Cook with you, parent with you, dance with you. Yes, I'll marry you." I laughed as he stood and tugged me up with him, pulling me into his strong, loving arms.

He pressed a tender kiss to my forehead as I breathed him in, tears forming at the corners of my eyes. Joyful tears. He cradled my face in his palm as he peered down at me with so much love and affection in his eyes, then leaned lower and kissed my lips, slowly, deliberately, as if he had the rest of his life to stand there and let me know how he felt.

I felt the exact same way.

As I pressed my body into his, his phone sounded with an alert I recognized as being from Sam.

Still kissing me, Chance laughed, then ended the kiss, pulled out his phone, and read his daughter's message. He laughed again and held it up for me to read.

Sam: *Well?*

I tilted my head, trying to figure out what I was missing. "Well what?"

Grinning, he typed something in, hit send, then showed me.

Chance: *She said yes!*

"She knew?" I asked, overflowing with laughter and happiness.

"Remember she's the one who set me straight," Chance said. "She helped me come up with the grand gesture, as she insisted on calling it."

He no sooner got the words out than my phone buzzed with a message at the same time his sounded again.

I reached to the bed, where I'd tossed mine aside, and picked it up as Chance looked at his. When I opened the message from Sam, my screen vibrated with a fireworks display and a message she'd sent to both Chance and me:

> Sam: Congratulations, you two! I can't wait to be a family of four.

Single Chance

We both typed into our respective phones.

> Rowan: Thank you for setting him straight! Love you.

> Chance: Thanks, Sammy. I'll be home a little later.

> Sam: Don't want to know any details!

Laughing, we set our phones on the nightstand at the same time. Then Chance lowered me to the bed and covered my body with his.

"The details," he growled into my ear, "are the very best part."

"I love me a detail man."

"I'm so damn happy to hear that, because this detail man is yours for the rest of your life."

Epilogue

Two months later

Rowan

Dragonfly Lake in the springtime was stunning as promised.

With my husband by my side, I breathed in a full, fragrant breath of the May evening and marveled that this was my life now.

Rusty Anchor's beer patio, bordered by lush, colorful flowers on two sides and a vista of the lake on the third, was the ideal venue for our gender reveal party. We'd closed it to the public for the duration, allowing our thirty-ish guests plenty of space to eat, drink, spread out, and enjoy the view before it got dark.

"This is beautiful," I said to Chance, whose arm was around me as we mingled with our friends.

We were minutes from sunset. The colors cast over the water ranged from gold and coral to a deep, dusky grayish plum. A bank of clouds in the distance increased the sky's drama without threatening our perfect spring weather.

"*You're* beautiful," he said in my ear.

Even though we were surrounded by our friends, his intimate declaration awakened a physical desire deep inside me I knew I'd be quenching later tonight.

I pressed a quick kiss to his lips, a grin on my own.

The joy I felt in my soul made it impossible not to smile, laugh, love, not only my handsome husband but all the people who'd joined us this evening. It was hard to remember how depleted and overcome with sadness I'd been when I'd happened into this little town five months ago. I'd lost everything then, and somehow I'd lucked into a life overflowing with friends and goodness and love.

In addition to Chloe, I'd gotten to know several of her friends, plus the dads in Chance's group, and the wives and fiancées of Knox, Ben, and Max. They were all with us tonight, as were Sam and her friend Kinsley, Loretta, Kemp, and the rest of the brewery employees. Magnolia from the Lily Pad had volunteered to help me plan the details, from the silver, pink, and blue balloons and centerpieces to the guess-the-gender board and the suggest-a-name station.

Chance and I stood in a cluster with Chloe, Magnolia, Emerson, Loretta, Olivia, and Anna.

"This looks fantastic," Emerson said as she bent over one of the tables to sniff the flowers in the middle.

"Magnolia deserves all the credit," I said.

"Aww, thank you," Magnolia said. "I had fun with it."

"I keep telling her she needs to make a business of her party-planning skills," Chloe said, nudging Magnolia's side.

"You really should consider it, dear," Loretta said.

"In my spare time between the Lily Pad and the inn," Magnolia said, laughing.

"You're good at event planning," Chance told her.

Luke and West arrived, and my husband excused himself to greet them.

We'd been married for three weeks. I was still pinching myself at my good fortune or fate or whatever deserved the credit for guiding me to that man. He was so exactly what I hadn't even known I needed. Forever supportive, full of love, humor, and common sense, and so damn irresistible. I knew pregnancy hormones could enhance a girl's sex drive, but I wasn't convinced those were to blame for how much I craved him.

Our wedding had been an intimate gathering of just over a dozen of our closest friends, everyone except Presley, who'd been too sick to get out of bed. We'd exchanged vows on the terrace of the Honeysuckle Inn, the exact one we'd discussed the first night we'd met. If you'd told me on New Year's Eve I'd be marrying Chance a few months later in that spot, I would've laughed hysterically and told you to shut up.

Afterward, our group enjoyed a private dinner party at the Marks Resort, prepared by The Cove's chef, Nola Simms, and her staff. We'd made the decision to branch out from Henry's with the good-natured blessing of both Holden and Cash, who were on our short guest list. I could understand why Nola and Cash had both received national recognition for their chef skills. Our wedding dinner had been unforgettable.

Though Chance had invited his parents and brother to the wedding, none of them had bothered to show up, claiming four weeks wasn't enough notice. Chance shrugged it off and declared it their loss. He'd told me Sam and I were what true family felt like, not the cold, self-centered jerks who'd raised him. I agreed. Those people, who I had yet to meet, didn't deserve to have him in their lives.

"You look gorgeous, Rowan," Quincy, Knox's wife, said as she came up and hugged me.

"No, you do," I said, grinning as I checked out her short, flouncy tangerine dress with boots. "I look like a plump blueberry."

Her smile was sad at the edges. "I'd give just about anything to look like a plump blueberry."

"You will," I told her.

"You absolutely will," Chloe said.

It was no secret Quincy and Knox had been trying to get pregnant. My heart went out to them. It must seem so brutally unfair that they could want a baby so badly and not be blessed with a pregnancy, and then someone like me comes along and gets pregnant after one chance meeting.

I squeezed her hand and tried to convey my empathy without drawing more attention to her.

Just then, Presley came bustling onto the patio from the parking lot, looking classy and sexy at once in a short, silver dress, thigh-high black boots, and a black cropped jacket.

"About time you got here," Chloe called to her.

"Hey, Presley," Olivia, the baker of the gender reveal cake, said. "Welcome."

"You look stunning," I said as she approached us.

"Thanks, Rowan. I'm sorry I'm late." Presley hugged me, then Chloe and the other girls in our cluster.

"There's no late," I assured her. "The food is about to be served, and we've got plenty of drinks, so help yourself."

"Yes to the drinks," Presley said. "I just quit my job on the spot."

I whipped my head to her to see if I'd heard her right. "You quit? Really?"

"Escorted off the premises and everything," she said almost flippantly.

There was a collective gasp, then Chloe said, "Well, good riddance."

Presley said, "Amen."

"What happened to make you quit?" Anna asked.

"I'll get you a cocktail. Would you like a Blue Bayou or a Watermelon Mojito?" Quincy asked, naming our themed blue and pink drinks for the evening, also Magnolia's idea.

"One of each," Presley answered, making us laugh.

"I got you," Quincy said.

"You seriously just quit?" Olivia asked Presley.

"She's needed to for a while," Chloe said. "Her boss is a douche wagon."

"She speaks the truth," Presley said. "But I didn't intend to waltz in here and steal the show. How's our resident pregnant lady?"

"I'm good even without the pretty cocktails," I said, laughing.

"This girl definitely has that newlywed glow about her," Anna said.

"That on top of the pregnancy glow..." Presley said. "You really do look alive and happy."

"I am," I assured her. "I'm truly blessed. And dying to know about your job."

"Ex job," Presley said. "So one of the partners is retiring. I told the douche wagon I was interested in going for partner. He told me not to bother, that I wouldn't get it. I considered my options on the spot—prove him wrong and get the position, or get that worm out of my life for good. He was so smug and self-satisfied and privileged white male, so...I told him what he could do with the job."

Quincy handed her a Blue Bayou.

"Thank you," Presley said, then closed her eyes and savored her first sip. "Walking out of that place with my box of belongings? Best. Feeling. Ever."

"You go, girl," Olivia said.

"Wow," Magnolia said. "Brave woman."

Presley waved it off. "Happy woman. Screw him. I decided on the drive here I'm moving to my lake house as soon as possible."

"Awesome," I said, meaning it. "You'll love it here."

Chloe laughed and shook her head. "It's almost like you planned it."

"Not consciously, but everything's working out," Presley said.

The servers from Henry's indicated that the food—an assortment of heavy appetizers—was ready. Holden took charge of encouraging our guests to fill their plates.

As people made their way toward the long table of food, Presley grabbed my arm and Chloe's and said under her breath, "Who is *that*?"

Chloe and I followed her gaze to the group of men standing near the bar.

"With the beard?" Chloe said.

Presley's reply was an affirmative growl.

"Down, girl," I said.

"Is he taken?" Presley asked.

"It's West Aldridge," Chloe said quietly. "Not taken as far as I know."

"Very single," I affirmed, as Chance had told me how anti-relationship West was after his last breakup broke his daughters' hearts.

The rest of the group meandered toward the food table, so the three of us gathered closer together.

"He's so not your type, Pres," Chloe said.

"I don't have a type. I rarely take time for guys, as you well know," Presley said. "But suddenly I'm feeling foot-loose and fancy free."

"Danger," I said with emphasis. "That feeling's *exactly* what got me like this." I pointed at my round belly.

Presley frowned at my middle. "It seems like it worked out for you, but I do *not* want an insta-family. He's just..." She shook her head, her gaze back on West.

"He's a contractor for Levi Dawson's construction company," Chloe said.

"Levi. I met him at your wedding reception, right?" Presley asked her, sipping her drink, looking nonchalant even as her eyes didn't leave West.

"Probably?" Chloe said. "I didn't take notes. I was kind of busy that night."

"Telling your new husband you were with child, if I remember right," Presley said.

"I don't know whether this will attract or repel you," I said, "but West is very dedicated to his little girls. And against any kind of relationship."

Presley looked thoughtful but didn't say anything.

"Your type," Chloe said, "is tall, thin, bordering on metrosexual, and brainy. The more expensive the suit he's wearing, the better."

My eyebrows shot up because West was the antithesis of that. He was former military, with a thick, muscular build. He was gruff, rough around the edges, and had a beard. I'd give her, he was good-looking, with intense green eyes that crinkled when he smiled, but he was about as masculine and virile as you could get.

"He's your polar opposite," I told her. Presley was wealthy, brilliant, and outgoing, while West was blue collar, brawny, and reserved.

Across the patio, West got a phone call and stepped away, letting himself out the gate on the lake side, probably so he could hear the call.

As the three of us made our way toward the food line, Holden came up behind Chloe and put his arms around her.

"Hey, Presley," he said. "Glad you could make it."

"I wouldn't miss it, handsome."

West came back to the patio, said something to Luke, then hurried out the other gate toward the parking lot.

"Where's West going?" Chloe asked.

"No idea," Holden said. "Probably something to do with his girls. I'm not sure what else would make him move like that."

"I guess I won't be meeting him tonight," Presley said and shrugged. She took a longer drink of her cocktail. "So what's your gut say, Rowan? Girl or boy?"

––––––

Chance

Life was funny. Not really in a haha way but more in a smack-you-upside-the-head-with-exactly-what-you-needed-even-if-you-couldn't-see-you-needed-it way.

How had I ever thought I didn't want *this*?

Rowan and I sat at one of the patio tables with Sam, her friend Kinsley, and several of our friends. I put my arm around Rowan and kissed her temple.

"Everyone's done eating, Dad," Sam said impatiently.

A glance at the food table told me it had, in fact, been demolished. Lots of our guests were standing, drinking, talking, no longer sitting at the tables.

"How long do we have to wait for cake, Mr. Cordova?" Kinsley asked.

"I think now's good," my daughter said.

While she wouldn't argue with cake itself, I knew my daughter's hurry was more about finding out whether she'd be getting a baby sister or brother.

Sam had made big strides in the past couple of months. Her friendship with Kinsley was partly responsible, I was sure, but so was Rowan. I'd always known, as much as I wanted to be both parents for Sam, there were areas I failed in. I just hadn't known what to do about it. The answer turned out to be fall in love with a woman who loved my daughter too.

We'd been cautious about discussing adoption possibilities with Sam, as Rowan didn't want to force herself on Sam as a mother figure too soon. When we'd returned from our short honeymoon on the other side of the lake, holed up in a beautiful vacation rental on the shore, Sam had surprised us in the best possible way by asking outright if Rowan could adopt her and become her mom. We'd wasted no time in starting the process, much to my wife's sheer joy.

Sam was less sullen toward me now that she and Rowan could talk boys, hair, and clothing to their hearts' content. I was fine being left out of those conversations and thankful as hell the sweet side of my daughter had resurfaced. She was set to finish her freshman year of high school with solid grades, a bestie in Kinsley, and a burgeoning business, as the two of them were starting a babysitting service this summer.

"Mama to be?" I said to Rowan. "Are you ready to find out what flavor kiddo we've got in there?"

Rowan shoved her chair back. "So ready. Let's do this."

"Yay!" Sam said, standing in a flash. "Come on, Dad."

Olivia, who was sitting on the other side of Kinsley, tuned in to our conversation. "Reveal time?"

"Yep. As if you don't know what it is," Kinsley said to her.

"I'll never tell though," Olivia said, grinning.

Olivia, who worked at Sugar, was the only one besides the ultrasound tech who knew the gender of our baby. The tech had written it down and sealed it in an envelope. Rowan had handed that over to Olivia, who'd agreed to bake the special cake that was filled with either pink or blue. She'd also baked the larger cake our guests would eat.

Rowan and I stood.

"Bring your drink. We're going to toast," I told my girls.

Sam practically dragged Rowan and me to the cake table.

The three of us had everyone's attention in no time, as "Is it time?" was repeated from one side of the patio to the other.

"Hey, everyone," I said. "It *is* time."

A round of cheers rang out, and though I'd not immediately embraced the concept of this party, now I was glad we were sharing our moment of truth with our closest friends.

When they quieted, I repeated, "It's time for the reveal. Well, almost time."

"Cut the cake!" Max called out.

"I'll get there, Coach Impatience."

Rowan stood to my left, and Sam was on my right. I pulled them both closer.

"I want to thank every one of you for joining us tonight," I said, as Rowan and I had agreed I'd do the talking. "I mean that. While the three of us can't wait to find out whether we'll have a boy or a girl join our family, we know that most of you just wish us a healthy baby, regardless of gender. But you came out because it's important to my family."

"Plus the open bar," Ben hollered, eliciting laughter.

"And the cake," Presley said.

We laughed with the smart-asses, then I sobered. "Some of you know I'm not close to my immediate family. That bugged me for years as I tried to figure out what was wrong with me and what I could do to be closer to them. I played with the decision to move away from St. Louis, where my parents still live, for a couple of years before doing it, worrying it would make us even more distant and maybe end our chances of ever feeling like part of a family."

My daughter leaned her head on my upper arm on one side. On the other, Rowan squeezed my arm, nestling in closer.

"No way could I have predicted that moving away would be one of the best decisions I've ever made," I continued, "but that's exactly what it was. If Sammy and I hadn't taken the risk of moving, I never would've met the woman of my dreams. Sam wouldn't have met her bestie, Kinsley." I nodded at the teenager sitting at the closest table. "We wouldn't have learned that found family can mean a lot stronger binds than blood family." I paused for a second to swallow down the emotion threatening to overcome me. "You all have become our family. The people who care. The people we love. So thank you."

I raised my beer bottle in a toast. "To found family."

"Here, here!"

"To found family!"

I clinked my bottle to Sam's soda glass and Rowan's water flute. We all drank a sip, then Sam stepped forward. We'd agreed she could do the honors of finding out what color was inside the cake.

She turned an empty glass upside down, hovered it over the small, all-white cake, then said, "Here goes nothing."

Rowan and I held on to each other. My heart was pounding at the anticipation, even though I'd be happy with either gender as long as they were healthy.

The excitement in the air was tangible in the moments of silence as Sam pressed the glass down into the cake. Rowan gripped me as if her life depended on it, and I had the fleeting thought that supporting her through labor wouldn't be a pain-free experience for me.

"It's a"—Sam blocked our view, so we held our breath for her announcement, as planned—"girl!"

With a squeal of happiness, she held the glass full of cake and icing up high to show off the pink.

A round of cheers went up, along with random comments and jokes, as Rowan and I pulled Sam into a three-way hug. My daughter was bouncing on her toes as she dropped a brief hug on us, then went to hug Kinsley.

"She wanted a girl," Rowan said, her grin splitting her face as I went in for a kiss. "So she can knit cute girl clothes."

"And you?" I asked once I could pull my lips away from hers enough to speak.

She shook her head. "You know I don't care. I just want *your* baby, whatever flavor."

With my arms around her and our bodies as close as they could possibly be while still clothed, her baby bump pressed into me, I said, "You've got my baby. And my teenager. And me."

"Sounds like the perfect family to me."

Bonus Epilogue

Late August, three months later

Rowan

I never thought this day would arrive.

The last week and a half had been indescribable, as if a meteor had crashed right smack in the middle of our lives. A meteor we'd named Lila Rose. Rose had been my dear grandmother's name.

Our girl had come early—way early. She was born four weeks and two days before her due date. To say nothing had gone as planned or hoped for would be spot on.

I'd been put on bed rest and hospitalized due to placental issues, because why would my body do anything the easy way? Eight days after I was admitted, Lila Rose was born via c-section, but that wasn't the end of the drama. Our six-pound darling girl showed signs of an infection shortly after birth and was rushed off to the NICU for testing and ultimately antibiotics before I was even out of recovery.

For the past nine days, Lila had stayed at the hospital and received daily meds. Once my four-day post-c-section stay was up, the hospital had managed to find me an unused room to stay in when I wasn't with my baby. I'd never been so grateful, because the thought of leaving that hospital without my newborn in my arms was unfathomable.

The gamut of emotions Chance and I had been through... I couldn't wrap my mind around it, let alone process everything. The moments right after her birth had been full of elation, wonder, and the most overpowering love I've ever experienced, both for my daughter and my husband. When her Apgar scores had been high in spite of her early birth, we'd been overcome with gratitude, relief, and so much pride for our strong little girl.

And then less than an hour later, a nurse had noticed Lila looked a little "off." I knew now how much that angel of a nurse had kept her alarm from us, not wanting to scare us prematurely. I'd been out of it from the c-section and all the emotions, and Chance had been awake for nearly twenty-four hours at that point, so we'd naively believed it was normal for Lila to have additional testing.

Later, Barb, the nurse, had told us she'd acted more on gut instinct than anything. We'd come to realize Barb's gut instinct had possibly saved our baby's life.

We'd been trying to swallow that reality for the past nine days while also attempting to not dwell too hard on it as our outcome was a happy one. Our bundle of joy and stress appeared to be healthy now in spite of both her early birth and her infection.

I'd never cried as much as I had the past nine days, a tear-filled mix of fear, anguish, relief, gratitude, and so much joy.

Chance had been by my side nearly nonstop those first four days, with me pushing him out the door late every night to drive home and get a few hours' sleep. He'd ferried Sam in each evening for a couple hours to visit her baby sister, after staying with me most of the day. The depth of his love had never been more evident. At the same time, I worried for him. He was burning the candle at both ends, being a rock for me, Sam, and Lila, and struggling with the same range of feelings I was. Add on top of that holding the household together, seeing to Sam's needs, and driving back and forth... It was too much.

Once I was officially released and Lila was out of danger, remaining hospitalized just to get her meds and be monitored closely, Chance and I had decided he'd return to work until she was released. That way his paternity leave could start when we were all home, when we'd no longer have the support of the nursing staff.

That day was today.

Lila Rose was finally on her way home with us.

In addition to a painful c-section scar on my lower abdomen, I had countless new scars forming in my heart and mind as I recovered from our ordeal.

I'd never longed for home and security so much in my life.

Each of the nurses on duty when Lila was released hugged us long and hard. We were one of their success stories, their happy outcomes. Gratitude didn't seem like a big enough word for what my heart was bursting with.

Then Chance secured Lila in her car seat carrier, and the three of us were on our way. Sam would meet us at home, as she had a regular babysitting job for the summer and would be done in the next half hour.

We walked out the hospital door, my arm looped with Chance's, Lila in her carrier in his other arm. The early September sun beating down was the most surreal feeling, as I hadn't ventured out of the building for nearly three weeks. There'd been days when I didn't care if the sun even existed as long as my baby would be okay.

I breathed in the warm air, overcome. Unable to find words. Chance seemed to be in the same state, as we made our way toward his SUV in silence, moving as one unit against a world that felt...uncertain.

"Let's see if we can figure this out," he said once we had the back door open.

"You don't know how to secure her?" I asked, panic surging up in me because I sure as hell didn't have a clue.

"Let's just say they've changed a bit in fourteen years. We'll get it though, won't we, Lila Rose?" His tone was gentle and loving, in complete contrast to mine.

"Did you practice?" I asked, climbing into the backseat on the opposite side to see if I could help.

"I did. We just set her right about here"—there was a click—"and there we go. She's locked in."

I exhaled, trying to calm myself, then tested it.

I hadn't had a chance to practice the car seat because when I'd been admitted to the hospital, we hadn't bought one yet. The truth was, we'd been completely unprepared for bed rest and an early birth. We hadn't even decorated the nursery yet. We'd planned to do it all that upcoming weekend when Dr. Shah had sent me to the hospital.

In hindsight, I wondered what the heck I'd been thinking to not expect a wrinkle to come up with my pregnancy. That was how my body rolled. I should've been ready for anything, prepared far in advance, but nope. I'd had a hard time deciding on colors and theme for the nursery and, it turned out, had waited too long.

"Do you want to ride back here?" Chance asked me.

I nodded as I fastened my seat belt, not taking my eyes from this little miracle.

Chance bent down and kissed Lila's forehead as she slumbered away. Then he stretched over her and kissed me as well, cradling my cheek for a moment and smiling, as if to say, *We made it.*

I soaked in that sensation of partnership, of coming through challenging times together, stronger for it but a little wary, as if another layer of naiveté had been peeled from me.

As he backed out of the parking space and drove us away from the hospital, I caressed Lila's tiny fist while she slept, needing the contact and the reassurance that she was okay.

Once Chance had turned on the highway heading south out of Nashville, Lila opened her eyes and looked up at me. Her blue-eyed gaze was beautiful and trusting and made my throat swell with love. I offered my pinky finger, and she clasped her hand around it as I'd been hoping. Something about that instinctual movement brought me joy.

This was her first car ride, but she didn't seem to notice. She locked her eyes on me, wholly unbothered about whether her seat was secured sufficiently, one hundred percent trusting that these two people would keep her safe and cared for.

Out of nowhere, that irrational pulse of panic that had been my on-and-off companion for the past two and a half weeks reared its ugly head.

"Chance, what if I can't do this?"

"Do what?" He met my gaze in the rearview, brows raised, looking calm and collected.

"Any of it."

Lila turned her head to one side then the other. Rooting, I'd been told. Looking for food.

"I think she's hungry," I said, my distress growing.

I couldn't feed her while we were driving. We were probably still forty-five minutes from home.

"It's okay," Chance said. "If we have to stop, we'll stop. How long ago did you feed her?"

"I don't know." I didn't know what time it was, what time I'd fed her, even though the nurse had made a point of reminding me about when the baby would likely be hungry again based on the schedule we'd had these past few days. All of that had been sucked out of my head. "We can't just pull over on a highway. It's dangerous."

"Rowan." Chance's stern tone caught my attention. I met his gaze again, took comfort in his calmness, his soothing tone as he said, "We'll figure it out if we need to. She's not upset yet. It's early. She might fall back asleep from the motion of the car. Relax, sweetheart. We've got this."

I tried to breathe through the anxiety. Told myself he was right. Calmed down slightly when another thought occurred to me.

"When are we going to fix up the nursery? We need so many things. We're not ready, Chance."

"The crib is ready. We have a glider. A full stock of diapers and onesies and spit cloths. The necessities. The rest is superficial. Everything will be taken care of. It's okay, Rowan."

"How can they send us home with this little being? I don't know what I'm doing!" I was on a panic roll now, all reason out the window. It was all just feelings, doubts, fears running my brain.

"How much do you love that little being?" he asked, still calm as could be.

I narrowed my eyes at him. How could he even ask that? "To the stars and back. Unquantifiable," I said, indignation creeping into my voice.

"Which means we'll figure out every little thing as it comes up. Because that's who we are now. What we do. We exist, in part, for our little girl."

Keeping one hand on the wheel, he reached back to me with the other, wiggling it to get me to grasp it. I did, taking some comfort from his touch, his strength.

"I love you," he said. "You're amazing. We'll figure it out."

With each pronouncement, I relaxed a degree, then squeezed his hand and let go, needing him to focus completely on the road.

"Breathe," he said.

I made a point of taking in a slow, deep breath, feeling my system calm a little more. When I looked at Lila again, her eyes were closed. She'd fallen back to sleep.

As I watched the rise and fall of her sweet chest, I reminded myself the nursery decor wasn't important. A healthy baby was everything. And we'd somehow come out with exactly that in the end.

———

Chance

I pulled into our garage, killed the engine, and acknowledged my profound relief.

How many times in the past two weeks had I parked here alone, scared, lonely, and unsure?

That was behind us. My girls were all home now.

"She's still asleep," Rowan whispered from the backseat, sounding awed and thankful.

Before getting out, I sent Sam a quick two-word text as promised.

> Chance: We're here.

I climbed out, closed the door gently, and glanced at Sam's reply.

> Sam: Everything's ready!

A smile crept across my face. Rowan had no idea what we'd pulled off. She was about to find out. I couldn't wait to see her beautiful face.

I opened the back door and helped Rowan detach the carrier from the car seat, showing her the release.

"Hey, princess," I said as I lifted Lila, and her eyes cracked open.

Rowan climbed out this side of the car and stood, peering down at our daughter as well. I put my arm around my wife and drew her into my side.

"Welcome home, Lila Rose," I said.

Rowan took my hand, and the three of us went inside together.

"No Sam?" Rowan asked in the kitchen. "Is she still at work?"

"She was supposed to be done a few minutes ago, but maybe something came up." I was pretty sure she was waiting for us in the nursery. I set the carrier on the floor, unbuckled Lila, and picked her up. "Let's get you two upstairs so you can feed her and rest."

"She's rooting again," Rowan said, running her fingers over Lila's soft cheek. "She doesn't even care about this huge event of coming home for the first time." She grinned tiredly.

"We'll have to tell her about it someday." Taking her hand again, I tugged her toward the stairs. "Nursing and naps."

"Mmm," she said quietly, following me up.

The nursery door was closed, supporting my suspicions about Sam. I let Rowan go ahead of me.

When she opened the door, Sam popped up out of the glider and whisper-exclaimed, "Surprise!"

Rowan's mouth fell open, and she pressed a hand to her chest as her gaze went from Sam to the room to me and back. "What?" She pulled Sam into a hug as she continued to take in the room. "What did you guys *do*?"

By the end of the question, her voice went squeaky with emotion.

"Do you like it?" Sam asked. "If you don't, we can start over."

The high-pitched sound Rowan let out could only be described as wonder, disbelief, and love.

With Lila in one hand, I put my other around my wife as Sam focused in on her baby sister.

"Can I hold her, Dad?"

I kissed the top of Sam's head and handed over the bundle of baby.

"You guys," Rowan said. "How did you do this?" She turned in a slow circle, taking in every side of the fully decorated nursery, her eyes big and incredulous. "It's beautiful and perfect."

"We've been a little busy," I said with a laugh. "Sam's been a rock star, working on it even when I'm not home."

"The mural..." Rowan went up to the two-wall painting. "Is it...? No way did you get Lexie..."

"We got Lexie," Sam said proudly.

"Would you look at this?" Rowan said to me, spinning again to take it all in.

I looked at the room through her eyes, as if I hadn't seen it before. It'd turned out even better than I'd hoped.

The plain walls were a pale lavender. The two Lexie North, Holden's sister-in-law, had painted for us, squeezing us in as a special favor, were covered with purple-gray tree trunks and branches dipping down toward the ground with leaves in lavenders, pinks, and white. Greenery and flowers in all shades of purple rose up from the ground, making the room look like a misty, magical forest.

On the plain walls were a series of prints in lavender and sea-foam green, of flowers and sayings about baby girls. The crib was a light maple wood that matched the changing table and glider, with lavender bedding. The room that had once been Sam's was now a cozy baby haven with no detail left to chance.

"I can't even..." Rowan said, tracing her fingers over the leaves on the wall.

"Do you recognize the color scheme?" Sam asked her.

With damp eyes, Rowan nodded. "It's the blanket I made."

"Since you couldn't decide on a color scheme, we used that," Sam said. "I hope it's okay."

"It's perfect. Stunning." Rowan went to the side of the crib, where we'd draped the handmade blanket she'd spent so many hours knitting. "The room," she clarified. "The blanket is imperfect in a dozen places." She laughed.

"Stitched with so much love," I said.

Rowan nodded and came toward Sam, Lila, and me, her arms outstretched. "Family hug."

"Our first one," Sam said as Rowan put an arm around both of us, and we all gently surrounded our newest member.

"First of many," I said, emotion rising in my own throat as I held on to these three girls who were my everything. "I love you all." I swallowed hard, my heart overflowing with gratitude and love.

"Me too," Rowan said. "Love you both."

"Samesies," Sam said, grinning. She pulled out of the hug enough to press a gentle finger to her baby sister's nose. "Love you always, little sister."

I met Rowan's gaze. Without words, our eyes conveyed so much. We were lucky and loved and proud of our daughters. I, for one, couldn't wait to watch a close relationship bloom between them. And I couldn't imagine how I could love this woman who'd blessed me with such a beautiful little miracle any more than I did at this moment.

Lila let out a halfhearted squall, a precursor, we'd found out, to louder, more insistent ones if we didn't get right on feeding her.

As if sharing my thoughts, Rowan straightened and headed for the glider.

"Dinnertime," I said to Sam.

Lila's next cry was indeed louder and meant business.

"Zero to a hundred in, what, ten seconds flat?" I said, handing the nursing pillow to Rowan and pulling a super-soft sea-foam green blanket over her.

"Okay then, Miss Thing," Sam said as she carried Lila to Rowan. "I guess we all know who's boss around here now."

My eyes met Rowan's, as I remembered all the times she'd taunted me by calling me her boss, before we'd given in to our feelings and made a go of it. I was pretty sure she was thinking about that too, judging by the loving, light-hearted look in her pretty eyes.

Rustling Sam's hair, my gaze still on Rowan's, I said, "I wouldn't have it any other way."

Note from the Author

Thanks for reading *Single Chance*! I hope you loved Chance and Rowan.

Next up is *Single-Minded*, West and Presley's story.

Contractor West Aldridge's main goal in life is to protect his three daughters from another heartbreak. The wealthy new girl in town who hires him for a remodeling project is off-limits times ten...so why can't he follow his own no-heartbreak rule?

If you missed the Henry Brothers series, you can dive

into book one, *Unraveled*! Find out how a marriage of convenience can test even the best of friends!

Find *Unraveled* in ebook, audiobook, and paperback in my author store at amyknuppbooks.com!

———

If you liked *Single Chance*, I hope you'll consider leaving a review for it. Reviews help other readers find books and can be as short (or long) as you feel comfortable with. Just a couple sentences is all it takes. I appreciate all honest reviews.

———

Single Chance is part of the Single Dads of Dragonfly Lake series, which includes:

- Singled Out
- Single All the Way
- Single Chance

Note from the Author

- Single-Minded
- Book 5, TBA
- Book 6, TBA

Also by Amy Knupp

North Brothers Books 4-5

North Brothers: The Complete Series

Or binge the North Brothers in audio:

North Brothers Audiobooks

<u>Hale Street Series</u>:

Sweet Spot

Sweet Dreams

Soft Spot

One and Only

Last First Kiss

Heartstrings

<u>Hale Street Box Sets:</u>

Meet Me at Clayborne's

Clayborne's After Hours

It Happened on Hale Street

<u>Island Fire Series</u>:

Playing with Fire

Heat of the Night

Fully Involved

Firestorm

Afterburn

Up in Flames

Flash Point

Fire Within

Impulse

Slow Burn

Island Fire Box Sets:

Sparked (books 1-3)

Ignited (books 4-6)

Enflamed (books 7-10)

OR

Island Fire: The Complete Series

Themed Bundles

Single Dad

Opposites Attract

Grumpy-Sunshine

Cinnamon Roll Heroes

Childhood Crush

Forbidden Love

Friends to Lovers

Coming Home

Musicians

Second Chance

Workplace Romance

Heroines Finding Their Path

About the Author

Amy Knupp is a *USA Today* Best-Selling author of contemporary romance. She loves words and grammar and meaty, engrossing stories with complex characters.

Amy lives in Wisconsin with her husband and has two adult children, two cats, and a box turtle. She graduated from the University of Kansas with degrees in French and journalism. In her spare time, she enjoys traveling, breaking up cat fights, watching college hoops, and annoying her family by correcting their grammar.

For more information:
https://www.amyknuppbooks.com

www.ingramcontent.com/pod-product-compliance
Ingram Content Group UK Ltd.
Pitfield, Milton Keynes, MK11 3LW, UK
UKHW050445270225
4779UKWH00006B/68

9 781955 573696